n or before
w.

e Freelance Journalist

31431

Titles in the series

Series editor: F. W. Hodgson

The Freelance Journalist

How to survive and succeed

Christopher Dobson

Cartoons by John Jensen

(f)

Focal Press
An imprint of Butterworth-Heinemann Ltd
Linacre House, Jordan Hill, Oxford OX2 8DP

&ᴄ   A member of the Reed Elsevier group

OXFORD   LONDON   BOSTON
MUNICH   NEW DELHI   SINGAPORE   SYDNEY
TOKYO   TORONTO   WELLINGTON

First published 1992
Revised reprint 1994

British Library Cataloguing in Publication Data
Dobson, Christopher
  The Freelance Journalist: How to Survive and
  Succeed. – (Butterworth-Heinemann Media
  Series).
  I. Title   II. Series
  070

ISBN 0 7506 0005 5

Library of Congress Cataloguing in Publication Data
Dobson, Christopher.
  The freelance journalist: how to survive and succeed
  p.   cm. – (Butterworth-Heinemann media series)
  Includes index.
  ISBN 0 7506 0005 5
  1. Freelance journalism.   2. Journalism, Commercial.
  3. Journalism – Management.   I. Title.   II. Series.
  PN4784.F76D63
  070.4'023'73–dc20–   92–5055
                                                  CIP

Composition by Genesis Typesetting, Laser Quay, Rochester, Kent
Printed and bound in Great Britain by Redwood Books , Trowbridge, Wiltshire

CONTENTS

INTRODUCTION

People have a funny idea about freelance journalism. They tend to think of it in Hollywood terms with intrepid reporters dashing round the world, living in luxurious hotels, winning wars singlehanded, conducting passionate affairs and every now and again crying 'hold the front page' and then dictating a few lines scribbled on the back of a cigarette packet. Some journalists, gazing into the unemotional faces of their VDUs, without an ashtray in sight in their modern, sanitized offices, banished by the accountants to the outskirts of the city they are supposed to serve, might well dream of such a life.

Some make a break for freedom, others have freedom thrust upon them and, clutching their redundancy payments, decide to go it alone, free from news editors and office routine, free to make their own decisions, free to do the stories they want to do.

Well, as Evelyn Waugh wrote in *Scoop* (required reading for any freelance): 'Up to a point Lord Copper.'

The first thing a freelance discovers is that he (or she) is even more closely tied to office routine and news editors although the routine is the freelance's own and there will be more than one news editor. The freelance will also have to replace the often loose discipline of the newspaper office, which tends to be indulgent towards hangovers and long lunch hours, with a strict self-discipline which allows no indulgences, for in the freelance world it is a question of: 'No work, no pay.'

It is not a life for the lazy. If you are going to be successful you will work more hours than you ever did working for someone else. If you are on a story, there is no news desk to phone to ask for someone to replace you because you have done your day's stint. The choice for the freelance is stark: stay with the story and get paid or pack up and go home with nothing to show for your efforts. The good thing about this situation is that it is your decision – remembering of course the bank manager, the mortgage, the school fees . . .

You must also find the time, the energy and the aptitude for administration. There are accounts to be kept and these are not just your expense accounts – although many journalists find them difficult enough to keep up to date. As a freelance you will need to keep ledgers for the income tax man and the dreaded VAT man. You will find that newspapers no longer dole out large dollops of cash to freelances using 'Mickey Mouse' names. After years of painful experiences with the Inland Revenue they now make payments directly into the contributor's bank account.

Obviously there is every chance of a payment going astray between the executive who buys the story, the managing editor who approves the payment, the contributors' accounts department and the bank.

Making sure that payments do not slip between the cracks is one of the most time-consuming aspects of freelance life and involves keeping impeccable records of assignments, work carried out, and stories published.

You will, in fact, be running a business and will have exactly the same responsibilities as other businessmen. Stripping away all the romance of journalism, you will be selling words in the same way as the greengrocer sells apples and the ironmonger sells nuts and bolts. That may sound brutal but it makes no difference to the bank manager or the taxman what you sell as long as your accounts add up and you do not spend more than you make.

There are other aspects of freelance administration which are more directly related to journalism. You will, for example, need to maintain a filing system to build up information on your chosen subject. However expert and knowledgeable you might be, you will still need to refer to facts and figures and even cull the stories of your rivals for material, a process which is called 'research', never 'plagiarism'. Unless you have an arrangement with a friendly newspaper you will not have access to such material and even if you are allowed to use a newspaper's cuttings library you will have to go there to do so. You will no longer be able to send a messenger for the cuttings or call the information up on your screen. You will have to rely on your own resources.

That need to rely on your own resources is the essence of freelance journalism for, if you have been a staff journalist, the moment you leave an organization to set up on your own you will lose the protective umbrella of a large company.

There will be no accounts department depositing the cheque every month; no warm, dry office with a canteen; no library; no legal department to save you from the error of your ways; no office car; no stationery cupboard; no paid holidays; no expenses; no Christmas party; and no pension fund. You are on your own. You are even treated differently in the office pub. You no longer belong.

This feeling of not belonging can be very demoralizing for a new freelance who has spent many years among the noise and camaraderie of a big office. It is surprising how much you miss office gossip. More importantly there is nobody nearby to bounce off ideas, no newsroom to go to for telephone numbers, no old-stagers' advice on how to write a story. Deep mental adjustments have to be made which are even more difficult to cope with than the physical changes.

One of the most difficult misapprehensions to overcome is the notion that you can sit at home waiting for the telephone to ring with a juicy assignment just as you used to sit in the newsroom waiting for the news editor to send you out on a story.

That is the way to disaster. The telephone never rings, or if it does you will probably be so desperate for work that you will accept any assignment offered you, however much you dislike it – and that is the very antithesis of freelancing

Instead, you have to sell yourself. You make calls, not wait for them. You badger editors with ideas and stories. You become an expert on certain subjects. You acquire a reputation for accuracy and meeting deadlines. You make yourself indispensable. And then the telephone will start to ring so consistently you will be able to pick and choose what stories you want to do, and that is what freelancing is all about.

If, after reading this litany of hardships and potential danger, you still want to be a freelance, read on. In the succeeding chapters I will attempt to explain how you can organize yourself so that you can enjoy the rewards of being a freelance. For me, the greatest of those rewards is the comparative freedom working for myself brings. Nobody can be completely free but being a successful freelance enables one to say 'No.' And that is freedom indeed.

1 ORGANIZING YOURSELF

Once you have made up your mind to embark on a freelance career you must decide what type of work you are going to do. This may sound obvious to the point of stupidity but it is surprising how many people drift into freelancing with no firm idea of how best to make use of their talents and knowledge.

For some, the choice is obvious. The sportsman who wants to take up journalism will normally aim for the sports pages. The retired officer will write defence stories, the teacher will write about education. These people are led into certain fields because their special knowledge means they have the background, the contacts, the interests which smooth their path and give news editors the ability to add them to their teams of experts, the people who can be telephoned for an instant reaction to a late-breaking story and who provide informed, intelligent copy. And, of course, their inside knowledge also produces scoops.

The trouble is that these experts have to learn a second discipline when they make the transition to journalism. Their loyalty often remains with their old friends and old profession which sometimes prevents them writing a story about which a non-involved journalist would have no qualms. At the same time their old friends may view them with suspicion, fearing that they will betray personal and professional secrets.

A pointed example of this problem cropped up during the Gulf War when former senior officers became temporary acting freelances to comment on TV programmes about the conduct of the war. It was felt in some quarters that by talking about the war with the benefit of their long military careers they would inadvertantly give away information of use to the enemy. They argued that precisely because of their military background they knew exactly how far they could go. Nevertheless their presence on the box proved infuriating not only to other soldiers who believe the Second World War watchword that 'careless talk costs lives' but also to the war correspondents in the desert who were prevented by military censorship from making factual reports about the events being freely discussed by the television pundits.

This is not, however, a problem which affects most people wishing to set up shop as freelances. For some the process will be the reverse of that discussed above, in which an expert in another field turns to journalism. In this case a journalist with an overriding interest in a subject which he cannot fulfil through a regular job will go freelance in order to satisfy that interest and at the same time make a living out of it. The dedicated angler who earns his keep writing about fishing must lead a life of pure joy. Either way, for the expert turned journalist or the journalist turned expert, the path is mapped out.

It is different for the average hack without any special qualifications. Will you write features and magazine stories? Will you take photographs? Will you stay with news and cover the courts or the Town Hall, providing a service for several newspapers? Will you become a district man (or woman), covering a certain area and known to news editors as 'Bloggs of Brighton?' Will you go abroad and be a 'stringer' known to foreign editors as 'Jones of Timbuctoo'?

Many factors may affect your decision – the work available, your ambitions, your ability, the competition, your responsibilities. They all have to be taken into account.

It may be that the freelance market where you live is already overpopulated with too many writers chasing too few column inches. In which case you must either find an unpopulated niche in which to specialize or cast your net wider, aiming your work at publications outside your area – or move.

The ambitious, with sights set on what used to be Fleet Street, will obviously be writing stories to catch the eye of the editors of the national dailies. It should be remembered, however, that it is no longer necessary to be physically present in Fleet Street. In fact there is not a national newspaper left in the 'Street of Shame'. Not so long ago a freelance could deliver copy to the *Evening Standard*, the *Daily Express*, the *Daily Telegraph*, the *Sun* and the *Daily Mail* in a gentle ten-minute stroll. Now it takes half a day by bus and tube.

It may be that your chosen subject, politics, the theatre or defence, for example, means that you have to work in London, but if not and you are not overly attracted by the bright lights you might just as well stay out of the big city and deliver your copy by the electronic methods of communication which we shall discuss later.

Feature and magazine work could well suit the woman journalist who wants to continue her career while raising a family. This sort of work is useful because it can be fitted in round the family routine and the flow of work adjusted to the demands of the family. It provides an income, maintains contacts and provides blessed intellectual relief from the household chores. It also means that the writer is ready to take up a full-time freelance career once her children are off her hands.

District work and local news is eminently suitable for the journalist who has roots embedded in local life, who has a pint with the mayor and is on first name terms with the chairman of the local football club. It is the job of such a journalist not only to feed the local newspapers with news of district activities but to relay worthwhile stories to the nationals. And when the big stories break, 'Bloggs of Brighton' with intimate knowledge of local affairs will be called into action by the nationals' news editors.

The foreign 'stringer' follows much the same pattern as the local journalist except for being based in a more exotic locality. In order for the stringer to survive, however, that exotic locality has to generate enough news to pay one's keep in countries which often have a higher cost of living than the UK. It is one thing to visit a place on holiday, fall in love with it and decide to set up shop there, and quite another to make enough money to enjoy the idyllic life.

These are just some of the choices open to the freelance. They do not only apply to writers. Sub-editors also freelance, and, although their work usually demands their presence in an office, the fax machine now makes it possible for sub-editors to work at home.

Most photographers seem to be freelances and they spread their talents across many fields from industrial brochures to fashion, sport to hard news. And, if times are hard, there is always the occasional wedding. Pride in your trade is all very well but when starting out as a freelance, survival, more often than not, is more important than pride.

So, after taking into consideration your circumstances, ambitions and abilities, you have made up your mind what sort of freelance you are going to be. The next question is: how are you going to set about it?

DELIVERING THE WORDS

It is possible for a journalist to operate with just a pencil and a notebook; or, if wearing an old fashioned shirt, even to write his story 'off the cuff'. Theatre critics dictate their notices from scribbles on their programmes in order to catch the edition. Sports reporters often have to send their copy with the game still going on.

Once when I was covering a title fight between Carmen Basilio and Sugar Ray Robinson in New York, the telephone system broke down and I had to write a round-by-round commentary by passing cable forms back to a Western Union messenger who flashed them at 'urgent' rates to London. When the fight was over I turned to thank the man sitting behind me who had passed the forms to the messenger. It was Joe Louis, possibly the greatest heavyweight of all time. He was delighted to have been of help.

War correspondents, presented with an unexpected link to their offices, will dictate what they have experienced in a great flood of words – and then not be able to remember what they have said. This is the very stuff of journalism. The adrenalin flows and you are on a high. But it is no way to run a business. You need an office and you need equipment.

Obviously, if you can't afford anything else the pencil and notebook will have to do until you can afford something better. In the end it is the words that matter, not what they are written on, but the pencil and notebook approach to modern journalism severely limits not only the number of beautiful words you can write but also your access to the rich fields of electronic news-gathering and production.

THE RIGHT EQUIPMENT

The basic equipment for a freelance starts with a telephone and an answering machine. It is self-evidently impossible to operate without reliable communications so a one-person operation demands an answering machine which can not only take messages but play them back by 'remote interrogation' so that you can listen to the messages without returning to the office (or to your home). Your telephone should also have a built-in facility for recording conversations so that you do not miss out vital parts of complicated stories and you are not left open to charges of misquotation. A portable telephone is a great asset. There is nothing more infuriating when you are trying to telephone in a story than to find every public telephone vandalized. A walkie-talkie prevents you losing your temper and time and enables you to stay on the job.

A pocket tape recorder is essential for making notes while you are on the story – I take one with me while I am walking the dog in case I should happen to have an idea for a story or a pleasing phrase flashes across my mind – and for making sure you have got the quotation right. You must, however, never leave the notebook behind or, ineluctably, your tape recorder will go on the blink.

There is another reason for taking a notebook. I find that if I simply put the tape recorder in front of someone I tend to lose the point of a story in the flow of words, but if I also jot down notes, I automatically focus on the high points and can 'fast-forward' the tape, cutting out the verbiage.

A portable typewriter is always useful but it is imperative to get a personal computer and printer as soon as possible. As we shall see in a later chapter, this equipment, allied to a modem will enable you to send and receive material and to tap into data-banks.

You will also need filing cabinets, a library of reference books, a supply of newspapers and the appropriate magazines if you intend to specialize, headed notepaper, a large diary, and a contacts book in which you will faithfully record every telephone number you are given.

One absolutely vital piece of equipment is an impressive invoice book with your name and address printed on every sheet, for while editors will often ignore your demands for payments, accounts departments rarely have the nerve to ignore an official invoice.

All this equipment has to be accommodated so you need an office and a desk. Many freelances work at home and that can be fatal unless they can divorce their work from the everyday running of the household.

DISCIPLINE

Self-discipline is all important. You must harden your heart against the children's demands on your time. A full day's work has to be done. A routine has to be established. For this reason the freelance who works at home must have a room set aside as an office.

Some people find it impossible to work at home. They need to 'go to the office'. For them, the ideal solution is to rent desk space in a newspaper which not only surrounds them with the ambience of the newspaper world but allows them to take advantage of the newspaper's various facilities. Some newspapers have special rental arrangements which include an office and the use of communications, libraries and data-banks but these deals can be expensive.

Many freelances work at home.

Self-discipline is again important if you arrange to work inside a newspaper for it is only too easy to slip into the habit of taking long lunches with journalistic friends and losing sight of the fact that their salaries are being paid while they are lunching but you are making nothing. If the temptation is irresistible it would probably be better to rent a room over a shop in the high street. This is not being puritanical, merely marking a potential pitfall on the road to freelance success.

I appreciate that young people setting out as freelances may be living in bed-sits and may be hard put to buy any of the above items of equipment let alone rent an office. In which case the pencil and notebook will have to do. If you have no typewriter then dictate your stories over the newspaper's freephone line. The public library will have the newspapers and reference books you need. Public transport and bicycles are not as grand as your own car, but they do the job. If you have the determination to succeed you will be able to acquire the equipment as you go along.

What you must have from the outset of your freelance career, however, is drive and organization. It is no use declaring yourself to be a freelance then sitting back and waiting for the telephone to ring with an exciting, well-paid assignment on the basis of your previous work as a staff journalist. You have to go out and sell yourself and your wares.

You must make contact with the people you think will buy your stories. Write to editors, feature editors, news editors, sports editors, anybody in a position to buy what you want to sell.

Set up meetings but make sure you go prepared. Do some research on the person you are going to meet and the person's organization. You would not want to offer a cigarette to a dedicated enemy of smoking, or offer a story on the evils of religion to a newspaper owned by a devout Christian.

Always go armed with good ideas which you have thought through and can defend. If you have had any work published, take your cuttings book with you. And for goodness sake, dress respectably.

Editors tend to be natty dressers these days and they do not approve of scruffy journalists. One of the joys of newspaper work is that you never know what the day will bring, therefore you have to dress to cope with all eventualities. Two days' growth of designer stubble does not help you sell yourself or your stories. Being a freelance might well mean that you are free from office discipline but you are not free from the disciplines of the market place.

You must get your name known, and your telephone number on every news desk list, but you must also get yourself respected as somebody who can be sent on a story and will not embarrass the newspaper and can be relied on to produce reliable, clean copy in good time. It is one of the facts of freelance life that reliability is of more use to an organization than erratic brilliance. Of course, if you are brilliant as well as reliable, so much the better; but, alas, there are not many of us blessed with both attributes.

BECOMING AN EXPERT

The best substitute for brilliance is a specialization. If for example a news editor knows that you are an expert on a certain subject, or, at least, more an expert than anybody on the staff, the paper will happily pass such work your way. There is nothing so comforting to the staff executive responsible for the day's news and features than to know there is an 'expert' on call. Conservation and social services are two modern examples of such specialist subjects.

The editor or features editor will not be able to give you this work, however, unless they know of your expertise. It is up to you to make sure they know. That is true also of magazines, supplements and the 'electronic media'. They all eat up material at a tremendous rate and they are always in search of the expert who can turn in reliable copy.

It is not even necessary to specialize in a subject, you might do just as well by specializing in a certain group of people. Suppose, for example, you live in a town which has a barracks attached to it. You could attach yourself to the barracks. Get to know the commanding officer, the squaddies, the families, become part of the establishment so that you are accepted and trusted. It will be the source of a continual stream of stories and if you make yourself the 'expert' on the barracks and the people who live and work there, news editors will automatically pick up their telephones and dial your number when a story breaks there. You can use the same technique with the local football team or, if you live in a 'company town', you can concentrate on the local industry which employs thousands of people and provides the economic life-blood of the district.

This will only happen, however, if you have properly organized your freelance activities. It is no use having the best contacts and the best stories in the world if no-one knows of you or trusts you to produce the goods. If you are going to freelance you must not hide your light under a bushel and you must keep it shining brightly.

2 PROVIDING THE BREAD

Freelancing as a way of making a living has all the excitement of riding a roller coaster, soaring to impossible heights and diving to unimaginable depths, wildly profitable one month and poverty stricken the next. There can be no better example than the military and foreign affairs specialists who monopolized the television screens and radio during the Gulf War. Everybody wanted them, anxious for their words of wisdom, eager to pay for their services. Then, suddenly, the war was over. They vanished overnight from the screen. The flow of easy money dried up.

If they treated their earnings during that hectic period as an unexpected bonus like winning the football pools and tucked it away or spent it on a grand holiday, all well and good; but if they had come to regard those fees as part of their regular monthly earnings and neglected their normal work, it would have been calamitous for them when the guns stopped firing.

Similarly, freelances who concentrate all their efforts on covering one long-running story, a strike for example, to the detriment of their day-to-day activities, will have a hard time picking up the threads of their work when the strikers return to their jobs. Not only does the bonus money end, they find that they have lost the continuity of their work and there is a long and unprofitable gap to be spanned.

The answer to this problem of maintaining a cashflow is to have a bread and butter job which generates a regular income and to stick to it whatever the temptations of short-term easy money. A bank manager feels more comfortable about your loan when he hears the regular smack of a cheque landing in your account every month. If you have a source of income which pays the mortgage and telephone bill it irons out the roller coaster and provides a certain peace of mind. You can still get your thrills but you know there is a safety net at the bottom of each dive.

The importance of having a bread and butter job cannot be exaggerated. If you do not have one do not become a freelance. Stay with your regular job, however much you hate it, until you have made sure you will be able to pay the mortgage and the groceries.

The simplest way of making sure of the bread and butter is to make an arrangement with a newspaper or magazine to work a certain number of shifts for them each week. Many newspapers cut their fully employed staffs to the bone and then find that they do not have enough people to turn out their publication, so that they are forced to re-hire on a freelance basis the same people they have made redundant. They still save on pensions, national insurance and all those other overheads that boost their editorial costs so that they make a profit even after paying the freelance fees of their former employees.

CASUAL SHIFTS

This applies particularly to weekly newspapers who do not need a full staff until the last two days before publication. A full day's work on Friday and a double shift on Saturday as a reporter or sub-editor for a Sunday newspaper provides a welcome bread and butter income.

This may seem the very negation of freelancing to the purist but it does provide a warming sense of security.

It also provides the freelance with access to the newspaper's facilities. The cuttings library, the data-banks, expensive reference books, all become available along with access to agency copy. A newspaper is like a gold mine which yields up its treasure for a freelance.

Shiftwork also brings you into contact with other journalists. You must never underestimate the importance of contact with other members of your profession. You need to know what is going on. Appointments to positions of power, the introduction of new technology, a change in editorial emphasis, there are many developments that may vitally affect your work as a freelance. A newsroom lives up to its name: information is exchanged, ideas discussed. It is like starting a car engine with jump leads, ideas which have lain dormant are jolted into life. So a bread and butter job on a newspaper or magazine on these lines (it is still a form of freelancing) not only brings in a regular income, it provides information, material and inspiration for your other freelance work.

If you prefer to do this sort of work for a magazine then the best arrangement is to accept a retainer in exchange for writing a certain number of stories each year. Paid monthly, this provides you with a regular income.

Some magazines, like the *Reader's Digest*, pay their top freelances handsome retainers in this way, enabling them to concentrate on producing a few first class stories each year. In exchange, however, the stories have to be precisely geared to the magazine's requirements and are closely checked and edited. Having paid their money, such magazines are hard taskmasters and expect copy precisely geared to their requirements. I shall write more about magazine work in a later chapter.

SERVICE COLUMNS

Another way of earning a modest but certain income is to provide a regular service on a certain subject: nature notes, gardening hints, motoring tips, agony aunt. This type of work gives invaluable training to freelances who aspire to writing a column. The fixed, usually small, amount of space given to such features teaches one to write concisely and informatively. There is also no reason why you should not provide material on the same subject to more than one publication.

RETAINERS

Another way of earning bread and butter money is to come to an arrangement with a publication under which it pays you a retainer in exchange for first call on your services or first offer on any stories you may write.

If the editor does not want the story or require your presence you are then free to sell it or yourself elsewhere while keeping the retainer. You will be selling a little bit of your freedom but in most cases the bridle does not chafe too much.

CONSULTANTS

You can also sell your services as a 'consultant'. This can encompass many things but usually means public relations work: manning a press office, or advising someone how to get their name in the papers – or how to keep it out. This has its dangers for the journalistic urge to seek and tell the truth is usually blunted by the quite different imperatives of public relations. You will have crossed to the opposite side of the fence and once over it is difficult to climb back although those that do often have a better understanding of how the world works.

COMMERCIAL WORK

Good bread and butter work can often be obtained from advertising companies and commercial printers who win contracts to produce brochures and company reports and can handle the design and the printing but have no-one to write the words. I once got a splendid assignment to Pakistan when I was hired by a public relations company to write a company report for Pakistan International Airlines. It was easy work, well paid and highly enjoyable.

Just think of all the pieces of glossy paper that fall through your letterbox encouraging you to buy something or join some organization or vote for somebody. They are all covered in words. Somebody has to write them and get paid for writing them. So, in the language of the junk mail experts: 'Why shouldn't it be you?'

This commercial work sometimes develops into lucrative contracts to write books about companies and industries, tracing their history and successes – and occasionally their failures – over the years. This is not work to be despised; many well-known authors are happy to put their names to such books.

If, however, the thought of such commercialism appals you and you are of more literary bent, you may obtain work from a publisher reading manuscripts submitted by hopeful authors. One of the advantages of this type of work is that it can be done at home and, given that you meet the deadline, can be done in your own time.

As you can see there are many ways of earning your bread and butter. Choose whatever is available and suits you best. There are, however, certain fundamental rules:

- It is vital to have some sort of regular income.
- It will not be given to you. You will have to go out and find it.
- When you have found it, do your best to tie it up with a proper agreement.
- Remember that nothing lasts for ever – especially in the world of freelancing; so never be surprised when somebody snatches your bread and butter away from you. Always have a second loaf ready for slicing.

3 GETTING YOUR INFORMATION

You have chosen the sort of freelancing you want to do and you have organized your bread and butter work; now you must answer the question that engages all newspapermen and women: 'Where do you get your information from?'

When working for an established newspaper this is relatively simple. The whole organization is geared to acquiring news. Reporters seek it out. The wire services pour in a flood of information from all over the world. Correspondents and stringers add their personal contributions. Public relations officers provide an often embarrassing amount of material. Most people are only too ready to be interviewed. There are colleagues ready to help and news desks eager to organize stories. There is a supply of newspapers and magazines and there are files of cuttings and reference books in the library.

Often there is just too much material. How different it is from being a staff journalist when you become a freelance and all that flow of information is cut off. When I decided to freelance I found it was eerily like being transferred as a correspondent from New York to Moscow.

In New York publicity was the name of the game. My desk was piled high with information people wanted to give me, the tape machines chattered day and night pouring out news, radio and television kept up a barrage of news and telephone operators all over the USA took pleasure in tracking down people I wanted to talk to.

In Moscow secrecy ruled. There was not even a telephone book and an application to interview somebody took at least a week for the Soviet authorities to process. The only information available was what the Soviet government wanted publicized. Press conferences were gatherings where foreign correspondents were given statements by government officials. There was no question of eliciting actual news. What was regarded as normal journalistic enterprise in the West was regarded as espionage in the Soviet Union.

It came as a terrible shock to someone used to being spoon-fed, even force-fed, information. Much the same shock awaits the staffer who decides to go freelance. You no longer have the newspaper's clout behind you. How do you cope?

I have already discussed the advantages of getting shift work at a newspaper office partly because of the access it gives you to a goldmine of information, but what do you do if this avenue is closed to you?

READING THE PAPERS

The first thing is to ensure that you keep up with the news. You must buy newspapers and magazines, or, if you can't afford to buy them, read them in the local library. There is absolutely no point in trying to sell stories which have already been fully covered or do not take note of the latest developments. This is not only a waste of time and effort, it also gets you a bad name with news editors.

There is also no point in firing stories blind at publications you have not read. You must read them to study their style, to discover what type of stories are fashionable. Do they run long features? Do they run only domestic stories? Do they already have specialists covering your subjects? You must know your market.

Reading also sparks ideas, a throwaway line in somebody else's story can prove the inspiration for a feature; but you will not get that inspiration unless you read the newspapers, watch the television news and listen to the radio. You must know what is going on in the world and how it is being presented.

REFERENCE BOOKS

You should also acquire a modest library of reference books. *Roget's Thesaurus* is a great help in looking for the right word and is one of the most valuable works in any journalist's bookshelf, however literate he or she may be. An encyclopedia, a dictionary, an atlas, a map of the local town and countryside are basic tools of the trade.

A *Who's Who* is invaluable and you can acquire slightly dated copies quite reasonably. An encyclopedia such as *Pears* and the *Writers' and Artists' Year Book* are among the many other useful works of general reference. *Whitaker's Almanac* is a mine of important information. Specialists will have their own requirements.

The *Diplomatic List* is essential for anyone wanting to write about foreign affairs. The *Directory of Directors* is equally essential for writers on business affairs. Cricket writers will need *Wisden's*.

Obviously it will take time and money to build up your own library. In the meantime most of the reference books you may need can be found in the public library.

One of the most neglected but valuable works of reference is the telephone book. Every freelance should try to get hold of the London directories as well as the local edition. They are stuffed full of information.

Once when a story was breaking about the mistreatment of Kurds in the Middle East a news editor telephoned me to ask if I knew of any Kurds living in London. It had not occurred to him that there would be Kurdish associations listed in the telephone book.

I told him I would ring him back, opened the directory and there they were. I was able to give him the names, addresses and telephone numbers of all the Kurds he needed. He was enormously impressed and paid me handsomely. I tell this story not to boast but to drive home a fundamental lesson: when trying to find someone, first look in the telephone book.

CONTACTS BOOK

This brings me to the one book that no journalist can be without. When first opened it is blank but by the time it is full it will contain a lifetime's work in names and numbers. It is the contact book in which you should write down the name address and telephone number of everyone you meet, who is likely to be of any help to you in your work.

Do not be fussy. Write them all down. The young councillor will be a government minister one day, the lowly third secretary will be a knighted ambassador, the local bobby will be a chief constable.

The loss of such a book would obviously be disastrous. I have known grown men weep over a missing contacts book. It is vital therefore that you keep a master copy in your office, preferably in a large looseleaf folder which can be constantly updated.

The new numbers and those that you need to call regularly should be entered in a pocket book which can be changed when it fills up.

You should also keep all the business cards that come your way. Enter the information the card carries in your contacts book but keep the card itself because its design often brings back a more graphic memory of the person who gave it to you and the circumstances of your meeting than the bare letters and figures in your book.

OFFICIAL CONTACTS

There are a number of publications which are useful adjuncts to your contacts book. The Central Office of Information which handles all government information publishes a valuable booklet giving the names, telephone numbers, fax numbers and office addresses of the 'Information, Press and Public Relations Officers in Government Departments and Public Corporations'.

It is stuffed full of information for the freelance and runs alphabetically through the government bureaucracies from the Advisory, Conciliation and Arbitration Service to the Welsh Office. It can be obtained by writing to the COI.

Another publication I find extremely useful is the *Hollis Press and Public Relations Annual*, a commercial publication which not only lists official and public information sources but also the names and numbers of people to contact for information in industry, commerce and professional and consumer associations.

Almost every public relations officer in the country is listed in its 1,200 pages. There are a number of similar publications; you will soon find which one best suits your requirements.

MUSEUMS

Museums must never be spurned as sources of information. Although they deal with the past they also provide background which explains the present. This is especially true of local town museums which can give young freelances an understanding of the physical development and mental attitudes of the place in which they work. It is very difficult to write with feeling and accuracy without such understanding. You might get the bare facts right but you could miss the underlying truths in your story.

Specialist museums which also have excellent libraries can be of great value. I find that one of the nicest things about such libraries is the eagerness of the librarians to help. They spend their days dealing with fascinating material which too rarely sees the light of day so that they are delighted when someone comes along intent on using the material they have so carefully collected and catalogued.

Starting my research for a book on the sinking of a German liner by a Russian submarine in which some 7,000 people died, I asked a librarian at the Imperial War Museum if he had any material on the incident. He replied 'I have been waiting for years for someone to ask me that', and produced a pile of material which eventually formed the basis of my book.

This museum is a delight not only for parties of school children who tour the exhibits but for the journalists and scholars who work in the reading room.

Not only does it have a splendid collection of books, it has an unparalleled collection of diaries, letters and boxes of private papers bequeathed by ex-servicemen and their families.

Many of them are never read after they are filed and when a researcher opens them up it can be like opening little boxes of jewels.

SPECIALIST LIBRARIES

Other specialist libraries are maintained by societies devoted to certain subjects. It would be vital, for example, for any freelance wanting to specialize in foreign affairs to join the Royal Institute of International Affairs, otherwise known as Chatham House. This elegant house in St James's Square houses a fine library of books, magazines and cuttings of foreign as well as British newspapers. The institute publishes books and papers on foreign affairs and holds meetings and seminars dealing with current developments.

The Royal United Services Institute in Whitehall deals with military matters in much the same way with an up-to-date library, its own publications and regular meetings addressed by senior officers and politicians.

These bodies will be too specialized for run-of-the-mill freelancing but they are examples of the kind of institutions which are storehouses of information and powerhouses of thinking and are available to seekers after knowledge.

The Public Records Office at Kew where government records are stored and released for public examination after thirty years should be on every freelance's list of places where knowledge is available. It is not perfect, for the records are 'weeded' for sensitive material and some records deemed too sensitive for public sight are held back for as long as one hundred years. Nevertheless, many papers relevant to what is happening today surface every year.

For example, anybody writing stories about nuclear power and the effect of nuclear power stations on the health of surrounding communities should examine those documents which reveal the extent of the Macmillan government's cover-up of the seriousness of the accident and fire at the Windscale, now Sellafield, nuclear power station in 1957. Eight hundred farms were contaminated by Strontium 90 dispersed by smoke from the fire but nothing was said officially for eighteen months and only then after a carefully orchestrated campaign of soothing lectures and articles about Strontium 90.

The extent of the cover-up did not become apparent until 1989 when papers relating to the accident were released for public viewing. With this in mind, it will be realized that the Public Record Office is invaluable not only for the information that can be dug out of its files but for its insight into the way the corporate mind of governmental bureaucracy works.

The papers, the marginal notes scribbled on them by ministers and officials advising what action should be taken and the resulting decisions provide a splendid blueprint, enabling you to plot the probable course of other, more current, stories.

The institutions that I have mentioned are only a few examples of the places where information can be harvested either by the examination of original documents or, increasingly, by projecting micro-fiche on to a screen or by tapping in to a databank from a terminal miles away, even from your own desk-top computer.

When you are starting out on your freelance career you should find out what research facilities are available locally, visit them, make yourself known to the staff and familiarize yourself with the procedure. It is, for example, worth knowing that you may not use pens at the Public Record Office. Only pencils are allowed for fear that irreplaceable documents will be damaged. There are, however, pencils on sale at the front desk for the uninitiated or forgetful.

FILING CUTTINGS

The other thing you must do at the outset of your feelance career is to start your own cuttings library. Do not throw away your newspapers once you have combed them for ideas and done the crossword. They are full of marvellous background material compiled by expert journalists at often great expense.

Foreign correspondents report from the capitals of the world, political writers reveal what is going on in parliament and the corridors around it, show business writers tell the secrets of the stars. It is all there, ready for you to use.

All you need is a filing cabinet, a pair of scissors and a tidy mind – something even the most scatter-brained will have to acquire to survive as a freelance.

Cut out the stories which you think will be of use to you and make sure you date and label them. There is nothing more infuriating than picking a cutting from your files and not knowing where or when it appeared.

Discipline yourself to doing this every day. It soon becomes automatic and you will find that you will quickly have a worthwhile 'morgue'. Do not restrict yourself to newspaper clippings, cut magazines as well. Type out pages from your notebooks and file them too. Do not scorn publicity handouts; they often contain valuable information.

In time you should be able to reach into your files and provide yourself with an immediate background briefing on any story you might be asked to do.

Such a system is of particular value to the specialist. Nobody can retain all the knowledge about one subject in their own heads. You also have to keep up-to-date with developments in your subject and books, while they may contain the sum of knowledge on a particular date, are often out-of-date by the time they appear. So the comprehensive, neatly kept and properly labelled cuttings library is essential. You will know that your library has reached maturity when news editors ring you up and ask what information you have on a certain subject. They don't even want you to write a story, all they want is for you to consult your 'sources' and they are happy to pay you as a consultant.

It is one of the curious aspects of modern journalism that despite having micro-fiche libraries and terminals for every reporter, news editors often prefer to pay a freelance as a 'consultant' to look at exactly the same cuttings as those contained in their own libraries.

One reason for this is that many modern newsrooms are understaffed and the news editor would rather pay a freelance than have one of his reporters spend a couple of hours reading the files. Another is that complicated stories are often given to young general reporters who are happy to credit a specialist freelance with an 'assist' for guidance.

I am not for one moment suggesting that your filing cabinet of cuttings should be the central pillar of your freelance activities. It is all too easy to get a reputation for writing only 'cuttings jobs'. But it is a very valuable support, providing you with facts and figures, quotes, background and a knowledge of what has already been written so that you do not try to sell an old story – or, if it is old, to write in such a way that it becomes news all over again. It is surprising how many stories make no impact when they are first printed but weeks, months later cause a furore because a change in circumstances makes them important or because the way they have been written and presented gives them an impact missing from their previous appearance.

All that I have written in this chapter concerns research, the acquiring of information already written down and available for examination. It is absolutely vital that anyone aspiring to be a freelance should learn how to make use of such methods and tools for they provide the scaffolding for the building of stories.

They are, however, only the scaffolding. The fine edifice of any story cannot be built by files alone, it can only be built by talking to people. The importance of having a full contacts book is not that you have somebody's number in your book, but that you are able to pick up the telephone and talk to them or visit them.

Never, ever, think you can write a story without talking to the people involved. No matter how clear cut a story may seem, danger lurks and opportunities are lost by being so lazy or so over-confident that you do not reach for the telephone. Often, everything that seemed set in concrete crumbles away in a moment's conversation while something that seemed mundane takes on a new and sparkling life with a few paragraphs of quotes.

Always remember that as a journalist you are recording instant history, and to do that you must talk to people for it is people who make history. It was not the Spitfire that won the Battle of Britain but the young men who flew it.

4 TALKING TO PEOPLE

An interview can take many forms. It can be a chat over the telephone, a few hurried words before the door is slammed in your face, an off-the-record background briefing which will be denied if it is reported, or an 'in-depth' affair over lunch and a bottle of wine. From the point of view of the person being interviewed it can be an opportunity to impart knowledge, an unwelcome intrusion, part of a political plot, a chance for personal publicity; but from the journalist's point of view, whatever form it takes, it serves one purpose; to elicit information. That information might be straightforward news or the last piece of evidence you need to break a news story, it might be a piece of personal history which puts a story into context, it might be contained in one factual sentence or it might be a long, discursive interview containing no hard news but in which your subject reveals the hidden depths of their character.

It is all information of one type of another to be recorded and used or kept for the future. It is not only what is said that is important but also your subject's demeanour, physical characteristics and habits. Is he left-handed? Does she grow potplants? Write it all down. An interview to a freelance is like a seal to an eskimo: nothing must be wasted.

How then does one go about extracting the maximum amount of information?

SETTING UP INTERVIEWS

Having done your initial research, you must now set up the interview. If your man or woman is important they may be guarded by secretaries and public relations officers so if you have the time write a letter; secretaries who think nothing of brushing aside telephone calls with 'I am afraid he is in conference' or 'Would you mind telling me the nature of your business?' are intimidated by letter-heads and rarely have the courage to ignore letters. A 'forgotten' telephone call is explainable, but letters and their duplicates are permanent and can be seen by an angry boss.

Give in your letter an account of yourself and what you want to do. Mention mutual friends and enclose a copy of a previous story which might convince your subject that it would be worthwhile to see you. If it is particularly important and the person is likely to be sticky, add a letter of accreditation from the publication for which you are writing the story. Follow up the letter with a telephone call. If your subject is unwilling, do not give up. Persist politely but firmly. Try to charm them – a humorous letter opens many doors and so does a mutual acquaintance prepared to put in a good word. If these approaches fail and the interview is imperative, become a piece of grit in their life, so that they will eventually agree to see you in order to be rid of you. But, take care, you do not want to be accused of harassment.

The first thing to do is to go to those files you have so carefully organized and do your homework. It is useless trying to set up an interview with, for example, a foreign politician if you know nothing about him. It is insulting to him and you will find that you are conducting the interview blind, unable to introduce topics which would put him at ease and lacking the knowledge that would enable you to guide the interview and ask the informed questions that would produce the answers you should be seeking.

So the first thing you should do when asked to interview someone is to go to the cuttings and the reference books to brief yourself on that person. If, for example, you know that the prim and proper civil servant chap you have been asked to interview on a matter of council policy had won a medal for an act of blazing gallantry in his youth it will not only give you an insight into his character but enable you to conduct the interview on a much more human basis. Similarly, if you go to see a grandmother armed with the knowledge that she was once a chorus girl, you can prepare your interview around that fact. Knowledge is the father of more knowledge.

If, for some reason, you have to undertake an interview knowing nothing about your subject except that you are supposed to ask certain questions it is always best to make a clean breast of your ignorance. Apologize, explain – 'the reporter who was due to see you has had a car crash' – and throw yourself on your subject's mercy. Do not try to bluff it out. You rarely succeed.

Of course there will be times when you have to make a deadline and it will be impossible either to set up the interview or to prepare adequately for it. When this happens you will have to 'wing it'.

This may involve 'doorstepping', ringing the doorbell of someone involved in a breaking story and conducting an interview 'cold'. Sometimes you get the door slammed in your face, a humiliation which, alas, comes with being a reporter. Most people, however, are astonishingly willing to talk if they are approached sympathetically. Style is everything in those first moments after the door opens. You have to have a finely tuned sense of atmosphere and a lightning swift ability to react to it.

If you can surmount those first moments of mutual sizing up and are invited in and offered a cup of tea, you are almost home.

HANDLING PEOPLE

The course of any interview will be largely dictated by the interplay of the characters of the people involved. Some journalists are aggressive in their questioning. I have rarely found this necessary. I believe each interview should be conducted like a seduction, people want to be wooed. I know one Fleet Street editor who, when he wanted an interview with Mrs Thatcher, when she was Prime Minister, or some journalistic concession which only she could grant, would arrive at number 10 Downing Street with a huge bunch of roses. It worked every time.

Softly, softly is the watchword. If you are dealing with ordinary members of the public or people in the public eye who may have had disillusioning experiences with the press, they will have to be reassured rather than frightened.

A friendly appearance, a soft voice, amiable chatter and an air of benign sincerity works wonders with people who are understandably nervous. Aggressive questioning frightens them and makes them resentful.

They can also be struck dumb by an intimidating display of recording machinery. Some interviews are so sensitive, finely balanced between success and disaster, that even the production of a pen and notebook may bring them to an end. My method is to wait until the interview proper has been launched and then to say something like: 'I have a terrible memory and I must get what you say right; do you mind if I take a note while we talk?' Only then should the notebook be produced and it may take even more gentle persuasion before you can start to use the tape-recorder. What might be an everyday tool of the trade to a journalist can be frightening to others. To ask permission to use a tape recorder also reassures your subject. It makes them feel that they are in command of the situation and it loosens tongues.

The aim is to encourage your subject to volunteer information rather than have it extracted like cross-rooted wisdom teeth. Gentle questions might bring rambling answers at first but as the interview settles down and rapport is established so the questions can be tightened up, the course of the conversation directed, until almost imperceptibly the subject is led to a situation where he or she is willingly answering questions they would not have entertained at the start of the interview.

The longer the conversation goes on, the more they will reveal of themselves, often without realizing what they are doing. The result can sometimes be devastating. Nicholas Ridley was forced to resign from the Government when he spoke his thoughts about Germany too frankly into the tape-recorder of the *Spectator's* A.N. Wilson in the course of a long lunch-time interview.

When you have got as much information as you can by the softly, softly approach it might still be necessary to ask the hard questions. There is still no need, however, to ask these questions in an aggressive manner. If they are asked amiably as a natural climax to the interview they can bring answers which would certainly have been refused at the start.

It may be that these answers will still be refused and the interview abruptly terminated despite your soft approach; you would, nevertheless, have spent enough time with your subject to gain the necessary background for your story which you would not have got if you had gone at the interview bull-headed.

NOTES AND TAPES

In this connection it must be remembered that if you judge it safe enough to use your notebook and a tape recorder, the book should be used not only for noting the highlights of the interview but also for what the subject is wearing, his or her mannerisms, the furnishings in the room, the titles on the bookshelf, everything that will enable you to present a rounded account, giving your readers not only the stark words of the interview but also enough descriptive, gossipy, detail to enable them to picture the scene and gain some measure of understanding of the person who spoke the words.

If, for various reasons, it is impossible to make such notes during the interview, write them down as soon as possible afterwards. Go into the nearest cafe or pub and think the interview through, writing down the background notes before you do anything else unless, of course, the story is hot and the deadline near in which case all you want is a telephone and, please God, let it not be vandalized. Even so don't lose the background. Write it down and put it in your files. You never know when it might be useful.

USING THE TELEPHONE

Simply because of the pressure of time in modern journalism and the way in which the telephone has become part of everyday life, many interviews which require only the accumulation of information rather than an insight into character are done over the telephone. It is still not as satisfactory as a face-to-face meeting because the subtleties of body language which add to your understanding of the story are missing. It is for example much easier for someone to lie over the telephone than it is when they are looking into your eyes. It is also much easier for them to put the telephone down than break off an interview when you are in the same room. Someone who bangs the telephone down does not make much copy but someone who abruptly terminates an interview in their own sitting room and ushers you out either politely or with threats, reveals a great deal.

It requires sensitivity and experience to read the message of the nuances in someone's voice over the telephone. Are they saying one thing but trying to tell you another? You don't know what is actually happening at the other end of the line. Is the person putting a hand over the mouthpiece and consulting someone else before answering? You are literally conducting the interview blind.

The other disadvantage of the telephone interview is that it rarely lasts as long as a face-to-face talk; there is less time to develop a rapport and there is no chance to smooth over a gap when you have lost your line of questioning. Where you can have a gap in a conversation in a room while you consult your notes or ask to use the bathroom, a gap of more than a few seconds on the telephone usually leads to an end of the conversation, for while someone might watch you consult your notes or take the opportunity for a break in the interview to do something else – make a telephone call for example – they will not so easily hang on to a telephone which has fallen silent. And there is absolutely no chance of those revelations which open up so deliciously over a long, bibulous lunch.

The Subtleties of Body Language

For this reason you must prepare yourself for a telephone interview with even more precision than for a meeting. Write down what you want to know and organize your questions so that you have them on paper in front of you and can tick them off as you ask them.

This does not mean that you should be more aggressive over the telephone, simply that you have less time to soften up your subject and you need to get all your questions asked without hesitation.

A little flattery and a plea for help is a good approach. 'I am writing a story about the new developments at your factory and I understand that you are the one person who can help me.'

That sort of opening usually brings the suitably modest reply: 'Well, I don't know about that, but how can I help you?' You are then off and running, you have established the ground and the subject expects a series of questions from you. Having asked those you have prepared you can then go on to ask others which arise from your conversation.

You may well want to make a recording of your conversation and this is simple with modern answerphones which have recording devices built in; but, remember, under British law, the device delivers quite a loud beep every fifteen seconds so that both parties know their conversation is being recorded. So, if your subject is nervous, it might be safer to rely on your shorthand. Whatever method you use, it is vital that you keep a proper record of your conversation, dated and timed and headed with the circumstances of the interview.

THE TRICKY SITUATION

Another form of interview is that in which the journalist is the victim. There are people who are well-used to being questioned and consider themselves a match for any interviewer. They usually have a message to impart for their own advantage, know what they want to say and how to say it and take the initiative in setting up the meeting. When you are invited to eat and drink at an expensive restaurant you should always remember Lord Beaverbrook's warning to young journalists: 'There's no such thing as a free lunch.'

It may well be that the story your host is trying to sell is perfectly genuine but the point about the lunch is that having eaten it something is expected from you in return.

There are also those men and women who have secrets they do not intend to disclose but, for one reason or another, need to give the appearance of frankness. The crooked company director who has been caught with his fingers in the till is a good example, as is the politician caught in a sex scandal. They cannot ignore the story, but if they admit that it is true they are finished and therefore they must find a sympathetic journalist who can be conned into giving their own version without digging too deeply into it.

These people can be very tricky to deal with. The philanderer will set up interviews surrounded by his loyal family complete with Labrador – why do they always have Labradors? – and simply deny everything while your photographer is taking pictures of him with his arm round his wife who is smiling up at him adoringly. It does not matter that she knows he is guilty and hates his guts, they have put on a performance and created an atmosphere of domestic bliss which will be difficult to dispel.

The crooked businessman's ploy is to summon journalists to his 'power' office, sitting behind a big desk with the sun behind him and his public relations advisers and lawyers at his side.

It is all very smooth and they may be charming but the scenario is designed to intimidate and the threat is implicit: put one foot wrong and you will be sued for every penny you and your publishers possess. In these circumstances you are rarely going to get anything out of them that they don't want to give.

The ultimate in the cover-up interview is the press conference. It takes a confident and adroit person to confront a room full of journalists scenting blood but if he pulls it off, slipping awkward questions, turning aside hostility with charm and an apparent eagerness to be helpful such a conference can create a groundswell of opinion in his favour. One of the advantages of holding a conference is that journalists who know more than others are not likely to reveal what they know to their rivals by asking injudicious questions. So the really damaging questions are not asked at the conference and the journalists with the inside knowledge who hope to ask their questions in private are often sidetracked: 'You had your opportunity to ask your questions at the conference. I am afraid I can say no more.'

One excellent example of this type of conference was that held by the traitor Kim Philby after Harold Macmillan, then Foreign Secretary, had replied to an accusation in the House of Commons that Philby was the 'Third Man' by saying that there was no evidence that he had betrayed the interests of the country.

Philby immediately called a conference at his mother's house, dispensed beer and sherry, answered questions with his customary charm and challenged Marcus Lipton, his accuser, to repeat his charges outside the House. He won over the press conference; even those who still had grave doubts about his innocence were disarmed and Marcus Lipton was forced to make a fulsome apology. Through his bravura performance at this conference Philby was able to avoid exposure until he fled to Russia from Beirut seven years later.

Philby was, of course, an exceptional man, a brilliant spy who wore a double life like a comfortable sweater, and I do not suggest for one moment that any of us are likely to be invited to many such conferences but there is something of Philby in everyone who tries to con reporters and they use the same methods: the bonhomie, the apparent frankness, the drink, the clever lie, the challenge and threat.

How, then, can you deal with the conmen? The best way is by surprise. The rules for interviewing now change. Instead of setting up a cosy meeting you must now catch your man while he is off guard, at home, in a restaurant, getting into his car where you can 'bounce' him. Apologize profusely but 'can you spare me a few minutes because there are just a few questions which we did not cover during our meeting in your office?'

You immediately have him at a disadvantage for, having invited you to his office or taken you to lunch, he can hardly claim not to know you, and in his hurry to get rid of you politely might just give you the answers you want. In these circumstances even a 'no comment' is tellingly newsworthy and if he loses his cool you have him on toast.

Another way is to turn the tables. Let your subject know that you have evidence of misdeeds and suggest a meeting so that he can comment on your evidence. This is high risk journalism and the greatest care must be taken to ensure that you have got your facts right. In these circumstances your subject should always be given the opportunity to refute your story. Using his replies might tend to lessen the impact of your revelations but it could save you a great deal of legal and journalistic grief. It will also help build your reputation as a painstaking, honest journalist with a safe pair of hands.

READING YOUR TEXT

The question of allowing people to read what you propose to say about them is a spiky one. I always try to avoid giving any commitment but some people with unfortunate experiences at the hands of the press refuse to give any sort of interview unless you first promise to show a copy of what you write about them.

One well known theatrical person goes even further by making would-be interviewers sign a contract setting out the terms under which the interview is to be conducted. Either you sign the contract or you get no interview.

Allowing somebody you have interviewed any sort of control over what you write about them goes against every journalistic instinct but sometimes with, for example, a complicated financial or scientific story it is helpful to allow them to read it to save you from schoolboy howlers. With general stories and features it should be avoided for it puts you under an obligation and tends to inhibit the way you write the story.

However, if it is the only way to get a badly needed interview, you might have to agree. In this case always make it clear that you will allow them to read the story only to check for factual errors and not to interfere with the tone of the story or the opinions you have expressed. You must also make it clear that you will not be responsible for any alterations an editor might make.

Even with these stipulations it is always best for the freelance journalist to avoid having his or her story read for if it is unfavourably received it could result in angry telephone calls to would-be buyers and, at worst, produce a 'stopping' writ preventing publication, which few freelances have the resources to fight.

WRITTEN ANSWERS

An unwelcome development in the art of interviewing is one increasingly practised by statesmen who hate the cut and thrust of unprogrammed interrogation. The Minister regrets, says his press officer, that he is too busy to set up a fullscale meeting but if you would care to submit your questions in writing, he will answer them, also in writing and perhaps 'You might care to call at my office where we could have our photographs taken.'

What this means is that he will never ever see your questions but they will be worked over by his public relations specialists who will provide answers of a creamy blandness which will mean nothing at all. The five-minute photograph session is a sop to you so that you will be able to prove that you have actually seen the great man. The assumption is that you will be so grateful you will publish his PRO's answers as if they were the tablets from Mount Sinai.

The courageous – or wealthy – freelance will refuse this stratagem but if you desperately need an answer to a question with the stateman's name on it you might have to go along with it. One thing is certain about this procedure: your subject will never be able to deny giving the answer even if never seeing the question.

It remains an unsatisfactory way of conducting a so-called interview, but at least while you are having your photograph taken you can note something of the appearance and ambience of the man – he really does wear brown shoes with a blue suit and he has cut himself shaving.

Alas, even this token nod towards real journalism is dispensed with by the latest development: the interview by fax. Questions are sent by machine and the answers come back in the same disembodied way. There is no feeling, no personality, just words appearing out of the ether thanks to micro-chips. This is one of the worst manifestations of electronic journalism and it is the fault not so much of reluctant interviewees but of lazy journalists.

Of course the fax is an excellent tool and it often elicits answers where other methods of communication fail, especially if your subject is abroad; but it is soulless and if a freelance, or any other journalist, is going to make a success of interviewing it has to be done face to face. With every interview you have to try to look into the mind and soul to establish the truth and you cannot do that by fax.

How do you get your news? By talking to people.

5 GETTING INTO PRINT

If there is one rule of freelancing that is worth obeying it is, never write a story before you have sold it.

Writing a story on spec and then touting it round newspaper offices smacks of the bargain basement and it demeans both the story and the writer. What you have to do is convince editors that they are getting copy hot off the word-processor written especially for them, exclusives if not necessarily scoops. The trick is to leave them feeling that you have done them a favour by allowing them to buy your work.

It may be, of course, that while you are preparing your sales pitch, the story will take command and demand to be written, flowing irresistibly to its natural conclusion. In this case all you can do is to not to let any potential client know it is in being, for if you do your bargaining position will be eroded. Show your professionalism by promising to produce it quickly but never allow your client the advantage of knowing you have done the work and are therefore committed to making a sale.

Another reason for not writing a story before you sell it is that different publications have different requirements and want their material written in a certain way. It is no use trying to sell a story written in *The Guardian* style to *The Sun*.

DECIDING THE MARKET

So one of the first things you have to do when you get an idea for a story is to decide where you want to sell it. Certain stories command more space, bigger bylines and fatter cheques from some publications than others. The peccadillos of a football star might well find a place in *The Guardian* but their natural home is in the tabloids who will pay handsomely for the titillating details.

On the other hand, a well-researched, worthily-written feature on penal reform will find a place in *The Guardian* but be turned down by the tabloids unless it is studded with some teasing nuggets. They will then pick out the nuggets, dress them up in tabloidese, and throw the rest away. Sometimes, with skill and luck, you can sell both types of story from the same set of facts. You may not like what the tabloid does with your story, but if it is going to break your heart, you should not venture into tabloid journalism. I find that the best way of dealing with this situation is to write the story absolutely straight, pocket the cheque and never, ever read the story as it is printed. That way both my bank account and blood pressure remain in good order.

Later, of course, when you become a rich and famous writer you will be able to dictate your own terms and stipulate that you will write it as you want to write it and that not one word may be changed without your permission.

PUTTING UP IDEAS

For the moment, however, it is better to make sure of getting your story printed. So, having decided on the target at which to aim the story, you put your idea to the appropriate section head – features editor, sports editor, news editor. Do not be shy about it. Remember that newspaper and magazine executives are always crying out for ideas. A full file of ideas and stories has a disconcerting habit of slipping through their fingers just before publication time and a trusted freelance providing a string of usable ideas is a great comfort to an editor. The editor may not even want you to write the story but will buy the idea from you to give to one of his own specialists – another reason for not writing the story before you have sold it.

The more likely course of events is that the editor will like your idea but will want to approach it from a different angle – you may think this wrong, but it is the editor's newspaper – which is yet another reason for not writing it before you have sold it. Make sure that you are absolutely clear about what the editor wants and that you can do it. If you can, get them to confirm what they want in writing. Take care to arrange all the details: deadline, length, style, news or features? It is a waste of time and work and wrecks relations if you submit something that is not wanted. It does not help the editor's temper and it means that either you will have to rewrite it or that it will be given to a sub-editor who might treat it less than sympathetically.

Always remember that you are in the business of selling and you must give the customers what they want. You must also deliver what you have promised. There are few things more infuriating for an editor than to commission a story on the assurances of a freelance that it could be done and for it to become apparent that the story is a mirage.

I remember a freelance who sold a three-part series to the *Sunday Telegraph* on the basis that he could get an interview with a Middle Eastern potentate. He was given a large commissioning fee, decent expenses and an air ticket but he failed to deliver the goods and it was left to a staff reporter to retrieve the situation. The freelance was never used again.

SYNOPSES

You must make your approach with these provisos in mind. Sometimes, if, for example, you are trying to sell a feature series, you will need to follow up the initial conversation with a short synopsis of your plans. This does not need to be elaborate and rarely more than two pages long. You start with a general account of what you plan to do and then go through the series, broken up into numbered paragraphs so that the editor can see at a glance what you are offering for the money. You should also attach an account of the logistics involved and an approximate costing of the expenses.

You must settle the question of your fee before you start to write. I will deal with this important but too-often neglected aspect of selling a story in more detail in a later chapter.

BLACKLISTS

If, despite all your efforts, you do not make a sale at your first attempt with the story, do not be discouraged. There are many reasons for an editor turning down a story which do not reflect badly on its worth – or on your ability. The paper might have something similar in preparation, it may have already covered the subject – although you should be aware of what has appeared – or the proprietor may have banned mention of a certain person for personal or business reasons.

It is silly to pretend that such things do not happen in our profession. When I started my career on the *Sunday Express* there was a 'black list' of people who had crossed Lord Beaverbrook and were never to be mentioned. The list, notoriously headed by Lord Mountbatten, was never written down but it was engraved on the minds of all the 'Old Man's' editors. The reasons for people being on the list were often unknown or surrounded in Beaverbrookian myth. Mountbatten, it was said, was head of the list because of the film 'In which we serve' with Noel Coward playing Mountbatten as the captain of the sunken destroyer, HMS Kelly. One dramatic scene showed men drowning while a copy of the *Daily Express* floated by carrying the notorious headline 'No War This Year.'

Freelances cannot expect to be privy to such proprietorial idiosyncrasies although the word will eventually trickle along the grapevine and you will learn that certain names are taboo at various newspapers.

TIMING

Whatever the reason for your rejection, you have failed to make a sale so you must take your story elsewhere, adapting your approach to the style of your next potential customer. Again, it is easier to do this on the basis that the story has yet to be written and sell it as an exclusive rather than write a number of differently shaded versions or, heaven forbid, carrying round the same increasingly dog-eared version which reeks of rejection.

If you are turned down three or four times you must take a hard look at your proposal. It could be intrinsically flawed; you could be selling it the wrong way; or, as is often the case, your timing is wrong.

There is a certain ripeness about a story. Try to sell it before it is ready or when it has lost its freshness and you will fail. You must try to find that day when it reaches perfect maturity and makes an editor's mouth water.

Let us suppose you interviewed Lady Diana Spencer and took a roll of colour pictures of her when she was just a young, aristocratic baby-minder. You might have got a piece in *The Tatler* or *Country Life* or one of the women's magazines; nice, reasonably profitable but instantly forgettable. Suppose, however, that you had recorded that interview and saved it and the pictures. The whole of Fleet Street and magazines around the world would have clamoured for it, waving their cheque books at you, on the day she became engaged to Prince Charles. You could have named your own price. In such cases ripeness is everything.

CONSTRUCTING A STORY

Putting such heady thoughts on one side, let us assume that you have sold your idea. You must now provide the words. You already know what you want to say and you have discussed with your client editor how he or she wants you to say it. Some stories write themselves; they flow, effortlessly, with a beginning, a middle and an end and they are a joy to do. Others are hard work and have to be painstakingly constructed, sentence by sentence.

It is always best to sketch the story out before you start to write so that you erect a framework and can see where your building blocks fit into the structure. These blocks are formed from your original conception of the story, your research, your interviews, your observation and your conclusions. The way in which you handle them will imprint your own personality and style on the story.

News stories will, of course, differ from features in their construction. I was taught by that great chief sub-editor of the *Daily Express*, Basil Denny, that the ideal news story could be cut back from the bottom sentence by sentence, whatever its length, until it was just one sentence long and still tell the story.

You could, for example, write a brilliant news story, 1,000 words long, about the death of Joe Bloggs, the former England footballing hero, but because of the pressure of news be forced to cut it back until it reads: 'Joe Bloggs, former Arsenal and England World Cup star, died yesterday, aged 64, from a heart attack while fishing near his retirement home at Hove.' All the essentials are there in one sentence.

WRITING FEATURES

You cannot do that with a feature which depends on a gradual revelation of the story to make its point. Writing features involves splitting up the building bricks and using them like a mosaic throughout the story to embellish, entertain and inform. A feature on Joe Bloggs using exactly the same material as the news story would possibly open with the story of how, as a young man, he spent an hour every night kicking a tennis ball at a target painted on the door of his family's outdoor privy.

Having decided, in consultation with your editor, what sort of story you are going to write you must then marshal your material in accordance with the well-known laws of journalism: Who? What? Where? Why? and When?

Answer those questions and you will have a story. As you gain experience you will develop your own particular style but, however brilliantly you write, those same basic questions have to be answered, even if they are disguised by fine words and elegant phrases. Any story that does not answer all of them is flawed.

PRESENTATION

The next thing to be considered is the physical presentation of your story. With a running news story this is mostly outside your control. You will know your editor's attitude to the story; you will know what aspects of it to look for and you will know the approximate number of words wanted from you. The rest is simply a matter of getting the facts over as quickly and accurately as possible. All you have to do is make sure that you have your Tandy with you or there is a telephone available so that you can dictate the story directly into the copy system.

If you can give form to the story so much the better, but no sub-editors, sweating on a deadline, want to wade through elaborate descriptions of the courtroom scene, they want to know the verdict. You can fill in the atmosphere later. Often a single word in a factual first paragraph is all that is needed to set the scene: the tense courtroom . . . the packed courtroom . . . the turbulent courtroom. It is not brilliant but it paints the picture with economy and speed. Put everything that needs to be told in that all-important first paragraph, and then, if you have the time, you can write the fine words.

It is quite different with a feature or a magazine series. Here, presentation is a large part of the battle since it is more likely to be submitted typed or as a neat print-out from your word-processor. If it looks good, well set out on decent paper, an editor may well assume that its contents are also good. If it is scruffy, hard to read, with scratchings out and bits inserted in undecipherable writing some editors will not bother to read it. The words may be brilliant but they will be 'binned'. You are selling and you must package your wares attractively.

With typed work or print-outs present clean copy in double spacing with wide margins. Leave plenty of room at the top and bottom and never carry over a sentence from one page to the next. If typed, make sure you have a good ribbon in your typewriter and that each page is clearly labelled. Put your telephone number at the top of the first page so that whoever handles the story can get in touch without having to search for the number. If the number is there they will have no excuse for not consulting you about any proposed alterations.

But of course increasing use is being made of electronic methods of communicating stories which cut out the need for putting them on paper. Some publishers prefer to work directly from writers' computer discs while modems flash copy over the telephone line directly into a newspaper's system. This does not mean, however, that stories can be presented in a sloppy fashion. They still have to look good on screen with accurate tabulation and paragraphing.

Sloppy electronic presentation is just as off-putting for an editor as scruffy copy. The medium may have changed but the message is still the same: presentation can make the difference between acceptance and rejection.

KEEPING A COPY

You must also make sure you have kept a copy of your story either on paper or disc, preferably both, for a number of reasons. In the first place it is quite astounding how many stories get lost. Modems send your copy whizzing into space, never to be seen again; discs are wiped clean; the system deposits your story in an unused file. You have to have a fail-safe system.

You will also need original copies, whether carbon copies or print-outs, if you are sued for libel and the case turns on alterations made in your copy. You will need them for rewriting in the fullness of time when the story becomes 'ripe' again for if a story is worth writing once it is worth writing again, or at least the basic facts might become due for another airing. You will need them for doing your accounts. And you will need them for filing as part of your library of background information.

6 FREEBIES AND THE FOREIGN FIELD

To my mind the best job in journalism is to be a freelance roving foreign correspondent. I suppose it dates back to schoolboy days during the blitz when I read Rider Haggard and John Buchan, and, later, Hemingway and Maugham by torchlight under the bedclothes while the Luftwaffe prowled overhead. After all my years of travelling, I still feel the adrenalin begin to run when I set out on a foreign assignment. Who knows what adventures lie in store?

Alas, it is also the most difficult job to sustain simply because of the costs involved. Air fares, hotel bills and communications fees add up to a frightening amount which usually far outweigh the income derived from covering the normal run of foreign stories. It is also by its very nature not a job that will bring in a regular income. It is, in fact, a way of life designed to give grey hairs to the most tolerant of bank managers.

It can be managed, however. The first thing to understand is that unless you are very young, very foolhardy or very rich you must never go swanning off into the wide blue yonder without getting someone else to pay your expenses.

This can be done by putting together such a good case for the story you want to write that your potential client, newspaper, magazine or television station, will provide your air fare and expenses and pay you a decent fee – not forgetting a cut of the syndication rights.

Once again, I must emphasize that this can only be done by careful planning. Just occasionally you may walk into an editor's office and find him (or her) despairing of finding anyone to do the very story that you want to cover. You cannot, however, rely on serendipity to fashion a career as a foreign correspondent.

You need to present your idea lucidly, designed to appeal to the particular publication at which you are aiming. You have to give some idea of the cost involved, and the fee you are proposing. You also have to convince the editor that you are a right and proper person to represent the publication and to spend its money.

Having accepted an assignment you owe a certain responsibility to the publication, not only by producing copy but also by behaving correctly. If you wish to behave boorishly while representing yourself, that is your problem; but if you have been given letters of accreditation your behaviour reflects on the publication which has hired you even if it is for only one story. This responsibility might prove irksome to the true freelance but it works both ways because the publication, having assigned and accredited you, should assume responsibility for your well-being as if you were a member of its staff.

BEING INSURED

It is important before agreeing to undertake any assignment abroad, especially in 'hairy' situations, to establish that you will be covered by the publication's insurance scheme and that if you run into trouble it will do its best to get you out of trouble and out of the country. Freelances on their own have neither the money nor the clout to do this.

All this may sound rather dull and legalistic and not at all in the ethos of freelancing but you will find it remarkably comforting when you set out on your travels to know that you are working under a measure of protection and that your retreat is secured.

FIXING ASSIGNMENTS

Well-organized, profitable assignments are what makes a freelance's life a happy one. Few journalists, however, can string together enough of them to make a regular living. Some US and European magazines do pay very large amounts for assignments stretching over several months and resulting in articles or series which are virtually books, but it is not until you become a truly 'distinguished' foreign correspondent or a recognized expert in a certain area that editors will automatically dial your number and plead with you to undertake such work for them.

An easier passage to foreign assignments for freelances is provided by the Sunday supplements which are great caters of feature material and whose writers and photographers are mainly freelances.

Most of the supplements employ 'commissioning editors' whose job is to find the right freelance for assignments where their main publication would use staff journalists or foreign 'stringers'. The supplements are also generally receptive to good ideas although they, unlike their main publication, tend to buy in stories which have already been written and photographed. Naturally enough they will give the best assignments to correspondents they know and trust. It gets a bit cosy and the circle is difficult to break into.

There is, however, another way for the would-be foreign correspondent to get abroad and that is to put together a package in which your travels are underwritten by a number of non-conflicting sponsors. It is here that the 'freebie' plays an important part in the freelance foreign correspondent's life. A 'freebie' is usually a trip to some exotic place for an invited group of correspondents organized by an airline in collaboration with a hotel chain or the government concerned in anticipation of favourable publicity. Obviously you would not be invited unless your hosts could confidently expect you to write a piece repaying their hospitality but that does not prevent you from making arrangements to sell other stories in which you do not have to mention them once you have sung for your supper.

Neither do they have to be travel stories although your hosts will no doubt not look kindly on you if you write a political story which causes trouble for them.

For example, it would hardly be politic if you accepted an airline's invitation for a week's junketing to celebrate the opening of a new route to some faraway place and you repaid the invitation by writing a piece explaining that the local Minister of Aviation was a corrupt crook. There is no reason, however, why you should not store away the information you have gathered for use later when you will not embarrass your hosts.

The disadvantage of this type of trip is that you have no control over where you are going and it usually includes semi-official functions, speeches and dinners, which tie you to your hosts and involve you in local politics.

I once went on a trip to Nigeria which was organized by a local company and which was fully backed by the government. It was designed to show what a good job the company was doing in fostering relations between Britain and Nigeria while the military government, which had newly taken over the country, wanted to display how progressive and democratic it was. We were shown every kindness and one of the ruling junta held a reception for us. However, our host company's rivals became jealous of all the publicity it was getting and the day after the reception, when we were supposed to be travelling up country, they arranged by paying 'dash' to have us arrested at the airport where we spent a miserable day locked up under armed guard.

Now that was too good a story not to tell – much to our host's chagrin. Then, some months later, when a rich Nigerian living in exile in London was rescued at Stansted airport after being kidnapped, drugged and put in a container to be flown back to Nigeria to certain death on corruption charges, the experiences of that trip provided a rich source of material for background features on the situation in Nigeria.

PERSONAL DEALS

The other type of freebie is the one where you decide where you want to go and make a personal deal, committing yourself to writing a travel type story in exchange for an air ticket. The advantage here is that once you have carried out your commitment you are a free agent and can write whatever you want without embarrassment.

Suppose, for example, you want to write a powerful series about the Vietnamese boat people in Hong Kong. Unless you were a correspondent of the stature of the late James Cameron few publications would foot the bill for the whole enterprise but there would be more who would be prepared to buy the series from you and contribute a couple of hundred pounds towards your expenses. Having sold the big story, it would not be too difficult to find publications interested in other stories; for example, the future of horse racing in Hong Kong under Communist rule or the fate of Chinese dissidents. In this way you can build up both your fees and contributions to your expenses – but you will still need to get there.

So you go to the public relations department of one of the airlines that operates to Hong Kong and suggest that you should write a story, either for the airline's own magazine or for placement elsewhere, in exchange for a ticket. If the airline agrees and you can arrange a similar deal with a hotel in exchange for accommodation you are home and dry. You have to take care, of course, that if you promise to place a story in a certain publication, you can deliver the goods; so that too needs to be negotiated. It's a bit like a juggling act keeping several balls in the air at the same time. You need to get the ticket in order to write the stories for which you have been commissioned and you have to sell a travel story in order to get the ticket and this all has to be accomplished without dropping one of the balls.

The beauty of this arrangement if you pull it off successfully is that once you have acquired the material to keep your part of the bargain, you can get on with the real reason for your visit and nobody else need know about the provenance or logistics of your assignment.

It is easy to sneer at the freebie as a form of bribery. Certainly, Lord Beaverbrook refused to allow any of his journalists to accept free trips. As we have noted, his often expressed dictum was: 'There's no such thing as a free lunch.'

TRAVEL WRITING

If it was necessary for reasons of news for an *Express* reporter to take part in a freebie activities, the paper always paid for fare and expenses; but that was at the time when the *Express* had foreign correspondents all over the world. Times have changed. In these days of financial stringency, even star columnists do not hesitate to acknowledge their gratitude towards the organizations which fly them and feed them. Thus the freebie serves journalists, especially freelances, very well. For instance, the whole field of travel journalism is based on trips provided by airlines, hotels and tourist enterprises. Writing about travel is an agreeable career in itself and most travel writers are freelances who combine their journalism with writing travel books. They are invited to visit places they would never be able to get to without the co-operation of their hosts and as long as they fulfill their obligation to write their travel pieces duly naming their benefactors, there is no reason why they should not gather information for other types of story. It is an excellent way for young journalists to find their way around the world, learning the basics of the foreign correspondent's trade.

Such trips may also be the only way political journalists can get into sensitive countries where the need for hard currency tourist trade is more important than the desire to maintain strict censorship. At the time when the Soviet Union was being very difficult about issuing visas to correspondents, travel writers were being waved through in parties of tourists. Similarly, the first reports to come out of Albania for many years were written by foreign correspondents operating under the cover of travel writers.

POLITICAL TRIPS

Conversely, countries with a political point to prove may also lay on official tours for journalists in order to boost their image. Such tours will, of course, be carefully stage-managed with 'minders' ever-ready to make the political point. Nevertheless, it is difficult to hide the truth from a group of inquisitive journalists as long as those journalists are not already committed to their hosts' cause or too befuddled by their hospitality. I remember being taken on a government tour of some Chinese factories and collective farms at the height of Mao Tse Tung's 'Great Leap Forward' campaign. It was the most depressing tour. It was obvious the campaign was a failure. The people were cowed and hungry, the factories were silent, the farms were growing hardly anything. Yet another journalist on the trip, his eyes shining, but blinded with fervour, could find nothing but praise for what was patently a disaster.

He saw only what he wanted to see; the freebie had achieved its ends.

There are various foreign trips available. NATO will take defence correspondents to view exercises in northern Norway; the US embassy invites selected journalists to tour the USA; the Israelis will organize a tour ranging from the Golan Heights to the Negev desert, a tour so hectic that in the end you will be begging for mercy. Not all such trips demand an immediate return in the form of a story; the organizers are sophisticated people who look for long-term results from their 'conditioning'. Whether they succeed or not is up to you, but what their trips can provide for you is the opportunity to soak up knowledge, make contacts and put valuable telephone numbers in your book.

It may be that you have spent an uncomfortable fortnight in Upper Gamba-land where some hopeful hotelier is trying to establish a tourist playground. The food might have been awful and the mosquitos the size of pterodactyls with appetites to match but when, a few weeks later, revolution breaks out and a group of British tourists are besieged in the hotel, you will be able to go to an editor and say: 'I know that place. The hotel manager's direct number is . . . .' You will then be able to provide a news story and a background feature.

GETTING INVITED

A freebie is never a waste of time as long as you use your time profitably getting around, talking to people, writing it all down. The only freebie I have been on of which I remember nothing and from which I produced no copy was a Scottish Tourist Board's tour of the distilleries.

The main difficulty in this field is getting yourself invited in the first place. You have to get on their lists. Make yourself know to the airline public relations departments, the public relations companies that handle hotel chains and tourism for foreign countries, embassy press officers and anybody else with the ability to provide a magic carpet. Try to get some pieces in the travel magazines and the airline in-flight magazines, even if it means writing about your own package holiday. Another way on to the lists is by writing travel brochures for tourist companies. The travel editors of newspapers and magazines also enjoy a certain amount of patronage and, strangely enough, often find it difficult to find people on their staff willing to go on a freebie, especially if it is a long way away.

7 THE STRINGER ABROAD

It may be that instead of being a home-based 'fireman' and rushing off to a trouble-spot whenever the alarm bell rings, you will want to specialize in a certain area: Eastern Europe, the Common Market, the Middle East. If you are going to do this properly it will entail much study. The history, geography, politics, sociology and, if possible, the languages of the area, all have to be absorbed. Every journalist must be flexible, capable of writing on any subject, but specialization demands more than journalistic skills, it demands knowledge of the subject and area. Who, for example, could pretend to write knowledgably about the Middle East without a working knowledge of Islam and its sects?

LIVING THERE

This is especially true if you decide to live abroad. It may well be that you have had a life-long ambition to live and work in a certain place. You might be drawn there by a friend, the offer of a job, the scenery, the sunshine. There are cities where specialists thrive; Brussels for experts on the European Community, the Vatican for writers on religious affairs, New York for the United Nations, Zurich for international finance. Nevertheless, wherever you choose, for whatever reason, once you have decided to work in a certain place as a freelance you must give yourself a crash course on your new home.

You must also set about acquiring the 'strings' that will provide your income. In order to survive a 'stringer' will need to work for a number of organizations – newspapers, magazines, radio, television, and news agencies – each with its own way of treating and using 'stringers'.

You should always try to make a deal by which they pay you a retainer thus establishing a constant flow of income which takes care of the bread and butter factor. Anything you do which is not covered by the retainer demands extra payments. The retainer does, however, carry with it the obligation that whoever pays it has first call on your services and so it is not really ethical to accept retainers from organizations which are deadly rivals.

Obviously the more 'strings' you gather in your hand, the more secure you are; but if you have too many they can prove an embarrassment. Suppose you are coasting quietly along and a major news story breaks. You will have all those organizations who pay you retainers quite legitimately demanding preferential treatment in your coverage of the story. Worse still: suppose the story is so big they send in their staff correspondents and camera crews and you are committed to all of them? Life could be profitable but difficult to manage with everybody demanding your help.

WORK PATTERNS

Most of the time, however, the situation is controllable, with you answering requests for stories, suggesting your own stories and looking after visitors from your various clients. Do not think that dancing attendance on visitors is beneath a journalist's dignity. The sub-editor you help through immigration might be editor next month and that dreary newspaper accountant who messed up his hotel bookings might well be in charge of your expense account.

It is, of course, imperative that you come to an absolutely clear arrangement about expenses when you first take up your string. In what currency will the expenses be paid? How will the filing charges be paid? Will they pay a proportion of your telephone and car costs? Will they pay all the expenses for out-of-town assignments? All these questions must be answered.

Answering requests for stories is usually straightforward. You simply do them and file them although if you are asked for the same story by different newspapers it demands some ingenuity in writing different versions despite the fact that the requirements of editors can differ considerably.

It is somewhat more complicated when suggesting a news story. The accountants' control of newspapers has become so strict that few papers now allow their stringers to file a story without it being 'tasted' first.

There are all sorts of reasons why a story will not make the paper on a certain day and so rather than have a correspondent go to the expense of filing copy which is not going to be used, an editor on the foreign desk needs a telephone call early in the day to discuss what you have to offer.

You have to be prepared, therefore, to sell the story and in order to do this you have to make a study of your various clients. It is not simply a question of aiming for the tabloids or the highbrows as you might at home. You are now abroad and your clients may stretch from Australia through the USA to Britain. What might make the front pages in Australia could be page six in Britain and spiked in the USA. A story about New Zealand tourists involved in a fracas in Greece would do well in Wellington but would not be considered in Los Angeles. Quite apart from the question of local interest – which is very important – there are certain types of story which are acceptable on grounds of taste in one country but not in another. You also have to consider the various time zones in which your clients live. Will the story be dead by the time they print?

All these factors have to be taken into consideration when making your offerings and it means that, once again, 'freelance' becomes something of a misnomer because you have to organize yourself very carefully, reading the papers and the local news agency copy, listening to the radio, following events, telephoning your contacts, deciding what stories you want to do and then telephoning your clients in time for their morning conferences.

Some stories are 'naturals' and foreign editors will be happy to buy them straight away, but they do like to compile their list for the day and receive the editor's blessing for it in conference and so it is likely that you will have to wait for a call back before going ahead with the story.

One of the advantages of this procedure is that you will not be filing stories 'on spec' but that any story a publication agrees to take becomes 'ordered' copy and so even if it is not used you get paid on a 'kill fee' basis. Remember: never file a story unless you have sold it first. However, if you think the story is a natural: an aircrash involving British tourists, for example, prepare it so that you can file at least the first few paragraphs immediately after you have spoken to the foreign desk. You will then have sold your story and given the sub-editors copy to work on. This is especially important if the story breaks close to edition time. If you get the first account into the paper under your by-line it becomes your story and you will be able to expand it in later editions as the news comes in.

THE LOCAL CONNECTION

Many stringers working abroad combine their freelance work with working for the local English-language newspaper.

Wherever you go in the world you can find papers like the *Times of Oman*, the *Jerusalem Post*, the *Nassau Tribune* and the *South China Morning Post*. They were mostly founded in the heydey of the Empire for expatriates, and their senior editorial posts are usually filled by British journalists some of whom become great figures in journalism. Kipling, for example, learnt his trade on the *Lahore Civil and Military Gazette*.

This arrangement has many advantages. A job, even a part-time post, on such a newspaper not only provides a bread and butter income, it provides a place to work, access to the flow of everyday copy, and involvement in the diplomatic, social and political life of the city. More doors will be open to a reporter accredited to such a newspaper than to a freelance who is not seen to be part of the local community.

With the local English-language newspaper as cover, the freelance can cultivate the various sources from which to gather information: the embassy, the chamber of commerce, the sports clubs, politicians, the military, the police, customs and immigration, hotels and airlines.

In a number of small countries the ruler is not outside the freelance's circle of contacts, although that can be a two-edged affair with the ruler expecting glowing reports of the country's regime in return for favours. Any criticism can result in the withdrawal of those favours, expulsion or, possibly, a spell in the local jail.

There are other dangers. Freelances can sometimes become too closely involved in local politics with different parties attempting to enlist their help to spread propaganda and disinformation. One night in Havana, just before Castro came down from the hills, I went out on the town with a local freelance who, before getting up to dance with his girlfriend, said to me 'look after this for me, will you?' and dropped something heavy in my pocket. It was a .38 revolver. He had managed to upset both the government and Castro and carried the gun as protection. He later achieved a measure of fame by challenging Ernest Hemingway to a duel, but it came to nothing.

Such braggadocio enlivens the scene, but it has little to do with earning a living as a freelance abroad in the modern world. Alas, the days of the buccaneering correspondent are long gone. You can no longer settle down in the city of your choice and start filing copy without reference to the local authorities.

VISAS AND WORK PERMITS

Every country in the world has learnt about the power of propaganda and the foreign correspondent is hedged about by rules and regulations. In most countries you must have a visa to get in and a work permit to stay. You must register with the Ministry of Information and only after obtaining your accreditation with its plastic pass may you file. You are subject to the local law of censorship and above you hangs the constant threat of being expelled if you offend the government.

You can attempt to circumvent the regulations by sliding into the country as a tourist and setting up shop, hoping that no-one will ask awkward questions, or by arranging matters with the liberal use of 'baksheesh.' This works sometimes but if rumbled you can also be thrown in jail and then out of the country.

It is better in the long run to go through the official channels and apply for a visa and a work permit. It would help if you could arrange a job on a local paper because the proprietor will then be able to apply for a work permit for you to join his publication. It also helps to make friends with the press officer at the appropriate embassy before setting out. A couple of lunches will be well repaid by help in cutting the red tape.

If you intend to work almost anywhere outside the Common Market you will certainly need;

- a large supply of photographs,
- proof that you can support yourself,
- a return ticket,
- the names of people who can vouch for you in the country in which you intend to work,
- a guarantee from a client that he will be responsible for your debts and behaviour.

Every country has its own regulations. In the USA you will need your Green Card work permit before starting work. In Australia you can work for a year without a permit but then you have to leave the country and apply for a work permit before re-entering. The only way to be sure of getting it right is to go to the embassy of the country where you want to work and ask for a copy of the regulations. Then find someone who has worked in the country and ask them about the pitfalls and the way round them.

You will find it helpful to consult the Foreign Office and discuss your project with experts dealing with the area in which you propose to work. They will not only be able to advise you on how to obtain visas and work permits but also give you a first class briefing on the area and provide you with some useful contacts.

Not so long ago many journalists used to avoid British embassies on the grounds that they were more likely to hinder than assist. At the same time the diplomats would regard journalists more as enemies than friends. Neither trusted the other.

A grudging invitation to strawberries and cream and not too much champagne to mark the Queen's Birthday was the closest some embassies got to co-operation with the press. Although there is a residue of mutual suspicion, these attitudes have largely disappeared and I always find it worthwhile to call on the embassy's Press Officer, even if it is only to get a glass of scotch in a 'dry' country.

You must also attend to the medical side of your new enterprise. Make sure your jabs are up-to-date. If you are going to work in any Third World country you will be exposed to endemic diseases. Hepatitis, Cholera, Typhoid, Polio, Yellow Fever and Plague are all

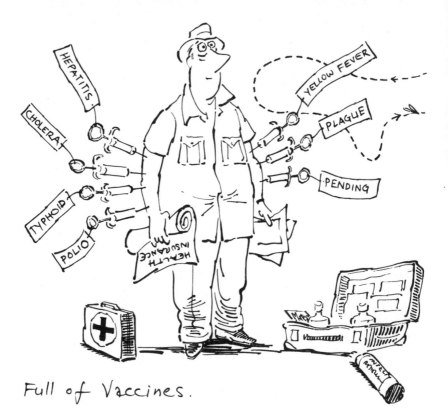

Full of Vaccines.

on the agenda. It goes without saying that unless you have the original cast-iron stomach you will be subject to recurring bouts of Gippy Tummy, Montezuma's Revenge, whatever you care to call it. And never attempt to pat a strange dog. They may not have pit bull terriers in the Far East, but they do have rabies. If you are taking any form of medication make sure you have a sufficient supply just in case it is not available where you are going. Some form of medical insurance is also desirable. It costs money to be ill abroad and as a freelance you will not be earning while you are sick.

PRESS CLUBS AND PASSES

So there you are, with your visa stamped in your valid passport, your work permit signed, your body full of vaccines and your strings all attached. You are ready to start work.

Before you can start filing, however, you must register at the Ministry of Information and obtain your press card. This involves letters of accreditation, more forms and even more photographs.

You may try to avoid giving yourself into the hands of the Ministry of Information (which in most cases belies its name) but there is little you can do about it if you intend to stay in the country. The ministry has the power to stop you working and you will find it very difficult to operate without the official press card. On the other hand, possession of the card often brings certain privileges like cheap travel and telephones. Being on the ministry list also makes sure that you are invited to government functions, press conferences and trips and receive government publications. Some governments also run press centres with free communications and pleasant restaurants. The super-moral may think this reeks of bribery but it is simply the way things work.

A counter-balance to the government press centre is usually provided by the local press club. There is always a press club ranging from the prestigious National Press Club in Washington to the Foreign Correspondents Club in Hong Kong made famous by John Le Carre in *The Honourable Schoolboy* and the uproarious bar above the so-called Diplomat Club in Harare.

Whatever sort of establishment it might be, it is vital that you should join for it is there that you hear the gossip, learn of the intrigues and listen to the dissidents and the trouble-makers telling the cynical truths far removed from the disinformation and platitudes of the Ministry of Information.

CENSORSHIP PROBLEMS

You may find yourself in a country which still has censorship; this is very boring because it entails taking your copy to the censor's office and getting it passed before sending it. With modern communications, Tandys and personal satellite dishes, you can break censorship, but your transmissions are detectable and the listeners can pull the plug on you. Also, if it becomes apparent that you are persistently avoiding the censors – they can, after all, read what you have written – you can have your work permit withdrawn and be kicked out of the country.

Sometimes the old methods are best. When I was a correspondent in Moscow every word that foreign journalists wrote was censored. We had to take our copy to the Central Telegraph Office in Gorki Street and hand it over the counter where it disappeared behind a green baize door. The problem was that we never knew when it was coming back. It could be a few minutes, hours, days even, before it was returned bearing the censor's broken arrow stamp of approval. Sometimes it would come back untouched, other times it would be torn to shreds.

Occasionally it never came back at all and that was usually followed by a summons to the Foreign Ministry for a warning about writing 'unfriendly' copy.

This censorship applied at the time to every aspect of Soviet life, We could not, for example, report that there was a shortage of white cabbage in the market. It was ridiculous. So methods had to be devised to get out sensitive copy. 'Pigeoning' it out, giving it to someone who was flying home, was one method. This had its dangers because unless the pigeon was someone you knew and trusted he or she might get scared and throw it away or simply not bother to pass it on at the other end. A much more secure method was for all the correspondents involved to club together to send a couple of their wives to Helsinki on a shopping trip. They would have a good time and be able to telephone the copy without fear of censorship. It was, of course, vital that when the story appeared it was not by-lined and not attributed to Moscow.

Foreign correspondents are no longer subject to censorship in Russia but the lessons learnt there are valuable for other circumstances. Israel is one of the few countries that maintains censorship in peacetime although it is supposed to apply only to stories dealing with military matters.

Sometimes, however, the Israeli censors get above themselves.

During the Six Day War, a number of university students reading English literature were drafted into the censor's office to cope with the flood of copy. One of them was given a story written by James Cameron to censor. Jimmy, who had turned freelance late in his career, was noted for the felicity of his writing. The student of English read the copy, pursed his lips, shook his head and said 'Well, it is all right militarily Mr Cameron, but it is a trifle banal.' We found Jimmy weeping. The same young man tried a similar tactic on Donald Wise, then writing for the *Daily Mirror*. Donald, a prisoner of war of the Japanese in the Second World War and veteran war correspondent, is a tall, elegant, but fierce man to cross. He seized his copy from the censor, crumpled it up, threw it at him and said 'If you think you can write better, go ahead.' (I have censored this quote.) The young man fled.

Israeli censorship in fact only really affects resident correspondents. Communications are so good that any reporter determined to get a story out will find little difficulty in doing so by pigeoning or flying out to Cyprus. The irony of this situation is that the Israeli media who are fully aware of the story can only use it by quoting foreign sources.

One must be careful about going to Israel, however, because an Israeli stamp in your passport will still bar you from many Arab countries. What you have to do when you arrive at the immigration counter is to say, 'Please don't stamp my passport. I'm travelling on.' The passport officer will then stamp a piece of paper for you to present when you leave the country. You must be quick, however, or his stamp will ruin your passport for travel in the Arab world.

You face a similar problem if you visit the Turkish part of Cyprus. The Greeks argue that this is territory illegally occupied by the Turkish army so a Turkish–Cypriot stamp in your passport will bar you from Greece. Infuriating obstacles like this can be set up overnight and ruin the most carefully planned assignment. One must always try to be aware of the latest nuances of national and religious pride and make the necessary adjustments.

Sometimes you just can't win. On our notorious trip to Nigeria one of my colleagues had taken some background cuttings with him. No objections were made to them when he arrived but by the time he went to board the plane to London they had become subversive and there was an ugly scene when customs officers insisted on confiscating them before allowing him to leave the country.

One of the first lessons one must learn on working in the Middle East is: which Islamic country will allow you to carry a bottle of whisky in your baggage and which will confiscate it at the airport. In the old days in Kuwait, 'travelling' whisky was ignored and if one ordered a whisky and soda at the hotel it was impeccably served on a tea tray. The whisky was in the teapot, the soda was in the milk jug and the sugar bowl provided the artistic flourish to the set-up. Now, one's baggage is searched at the airport and anything alcoholic is confiscated. I have often wondered what happens to the confiscated bottles. Are they smashed or could they find their way on to the 'black label' market?

Mindless bureaucracy laced with nationalism is one of the major problems you will face as a foreign correspondent. The only answer to it is tolerance and patience. It may be hard to keep your temper when some pipsqueak official keeps you standing in the sun while your story disappears over the horizon, but the moment you lose your temper and start shouting insults you are finished. Arrogance will get you nowhere. On the other hand 'dash' or 'baksheesh' or a 'tip' may work wonders. What might be looked on as bribery in Europe is simply a straightforward commercial transaction in other parts of the world.

It has always amused me that a man who would throw up his hands in horror when a few dollars are slipped into a minor official's hand to smooth a path will happily accept an expensive meal at a smart restaurant to discuss 'the unfortunate problems which have arisen . . .'

You have to be very careful to keep up with the local nuances, however, for every so often there will be a purge on corruption and the smiling border guard who gratefully accepted – or even demanded – his 'dash' the day before might turn overnight into an outraged upholder of morality, refuse your money with a great show of indignation and lecture you on the evils of bribery. A few days later, when the heat is off, he will settle back into his normal smiling, bribable self.

It can sometimes get more serious than that for 'corruption', although part of daily life in many countries is usually officially illegal, and can be used by governments to expel or imprison correspondents who have become a nuisance. So you must keep your nostrils twitching for the first faint whiff of the double-cross.

TRAVELLING ON

One of the first things you have to do when you arrive at your foreign outpost is to make preparations to leave it again. It is one of the laws of journalism that, for the foreign correspondent anything interesting always happens in the next-door country.

This, combined with the tendency of homeside news executives to look at a map and say 'it's only an inch away' ignoring the fact that the inch covers many miles of jungles, mountains and rivers, means that you will have to be prepared to fly off on the first available plane. It also means that if you are operating almost anywhere in the Third World or Eastern Europe you will need a visa. In many countries, especially in the Middle East, you can take a chance on getting a transit visa when you arrive at your destination; but if they are being awkward you may find yourself spending the night at the airport and being put on the first plane out. In any case a transit visa is usually good for only twenty-four hours. So it is best to keep your passport stocked with multiple-entry visas for the countries you are most likely to visit. It is also imperative that you have a visa which enables you to return to the country in which you have set up shop. Few things are more embarrassing than being refused re-entry into the country where you have a home, office and all your possessions.

It is also important to make connections with the hotel managers in the cities in your area so that a telephone call will reserve you a room and a welcome. It is one of the curiosities of foreign correspondents that, rather like migratory birds, they always seem to find their way to the same hotel.

Nobody quite knows how it happens. It could be a friendly management, a strategic position, a good bar, communications that work; somehow, the instincts of the foreign correspondents guide them there. Some such places have become part of journalistic history. The Commodore in Beirut, the Dan in Tel Aviv, the Intercontinental in Amman, are among those hotels which played a major role in the coverage of the Middle East. Some go out of their way to look after foreign correspondents. In Cyprus during the EOKA campaign the Ledra Palace Hotel had a hall porter called Savvas who was an expert at doing expenses. He would present a detailed account for lazy correspondents to send to their newspapers. His work, noted for its imagination, was paid for with a percentage of the expenses.

So, if a big story breaks, you want to be sure you have a room reserved in the correspondents' preferred hotel. You also need to have a bag packed, ready to go. There is no point in wasting time packing a suitcase and missing the plane or, alternatively, catching the plane and having none of your gear with you. Your case should be small enough to carry on. You do not want to waste time at the other end waiting for it to be unloaded from the luggage hold. It may be tempting to use just slacks and shirts as your travelling gear but it always pays to have a light, washable suit because you never know when your assignment is going to lead you into a situation where you need to be properly dressed.

Always make sure that you are properly shaved or your beard properly trimmed. A government minister or business tycoon will react more favourably to a well-dressed, clean interviewer than a scruffy individual in jeans. The same rule applies of course to women correspondents; a couple of light dresses and a travelling iron works wonders.

I do not, however, suggest anybody goes as far as I did at the beginning of my career when I used to take a dinner jacket with me. It came in very useful in Cyprus during the EOKA emergency when the Governor General, then Sir Hugh Foot, invited individual correspondents to dinner. He was surprised at the immaculate appearance of his guests, never realizing that they all wore the same suit, hitched up, let down and pinned to fit the shapes of the variously sized correspondents. Nevertheless there is never any excuse for not being properly dressed whatever the circumstances. Jeans and sweatshirts are fine in the field but not at the dinner table.

ORGANIZING YOUR COMMUNICATIONS

The last, and possibly the most important precaution you must take before setting out on an assignment is to ensure that you have your communications organized. It is no use whatsoever having the most magnificent scoop if you cannot send it to your newspaper.

This may seem belt and braces advice when modern electronics can put you in touch with your office thousands of miles away in a matter of seconds by half a dozen different methods and routes and some correspondents carry their own satellite dishes with them. But what happens when the electrical grid is blown up, when sunspots black out radio signals, when the revolutionaries seize control of all communications?

Getting your story out then becomes a test of ingenuity and initiative. My experience of these situations goes back to the days when you had to file by cable, sometimes at half a crown a word – a very expensive business which taught one to write concise copy. Cable offices also would close down at six o'clock and any copy not sent by then would have to wait till the following morning.

Why not telephone? Because international calls sometimes took hours to come through, were expensive and often incomprehensible. When the telex machine first came into operation, out of date though it now is, it revolutionized the lives of foreign correspondents. Journalists who learnt how to work the machines gained a tremendous advantage over their rivals.

At the end of the first day of the Six Day War, I found myself in the King David Hotel in Jerusalem with Robin Stafford of the *Daily Express* and Donald Wise of the *Daily Mirror*. We had marvellous stories to tell but no way of getting them out. The streets outside were being lashed by bullets. The telephone was down. Robin, a wizard on the telex, found the machine on which clients booked their rooms. He was told it would not work. 'It will, if you plug it in', he said and did so. It lit up like a Christmas tree and within minutes we were sending the first eye-witness stories of the war to London.

I tell you this to illustrate the fact that you have to be prepared for a complete breakdown in communications and it will serve you well to work out alternatives. 'Pigeoning' which I have referred to earlier, is one way. If you are with a cooperative group of journalists, one member may be volunteered to take out everybody's copy while the rest cover for the 'volunteer'. It is the modern equivalent of the runner with the message in a cleft stick.

Sometimes, as with the King David episode, commercial communications remain open when press links are cut. If you can, set up a fall-back arrangement with a private fax or telephone before you set out on the assignment.

In special circumstances embassies can be persuaded to send messages on their private communications systems which are not reliant on local power. These messages can rarely be more than 200 words long but a short story is better than no story at all and it is marvellous training in the economical use of words.

Some embassies are more eager to help than others. The French and the US embassies are particularly helpful to their countries' journalists. As might be expected, however, it takes exceptional circumstances for the Foreign Office to come to the aid of British journalists. Nevertheless, British correspondents remember with gratitude the wireless operator at the British Embassy in Amman who sent out their stories during 'Black September' in 1970 when fighting raged in the Jordanian capital between the Palestinian 'fedayeen' and King Hussein's Bedouin soldiers.

In more modern times, imagine the rage of correspondents in Baghdad during the Gulf War when their colleagues refused them permission to use their satellite telephones and they were left with no means of communication.

So, before you set out on a story do make sure that you have some means of sending your copy back. And remember that your editors don't care about your technical problems. They want your copy, not your excuses.

8 COVERING WARS

For some freelances all forms of journalism appear tame alongside the dangers and exhilaration of covering a war. You find them marching towards the sound of the guns wherever a conflict erupts into violence: veterans of a dozen wars who fret not when dodging bullets and young men and women thirsty for adventure and as anxious as soldiers to make their names on the battlefield.

If that is your aim in life, I would not attempt to dissuade you for it is my belief that to be a respected war correspondent is the pinnacle of a journalistic career. There are, however, certain lessons that must be absorbed before you even think of getting within range of the guns. The first is very simple: a dead correspondent is a bad correspondent.

This may sound simplistic but it is a lesson that every correspondent has to learn over and over again. It is all too easy to become over-familiar with death and to start taking risks which have nothing to do with journalism. You are not there to be a hero but to report what is going on to the newspaper which has hired you to inform its readers about the war.

The man who goes into the firing line every day does not necessarily do the best job for his newspaper. The danger is that you begin to judge yourself in terms of your own courage – or foolhardiness – rather than by the stories you write. You develop the 'firefight syndrome', a sickness that often ends in professional and personal disaster.

LESSONS OF VIETNAM

This sickness reached epidemic proportions in Vietnam. The trouble there was that the war was right on the hotel doorstep. During the

Tet offensive of 1968, correspondents could step out of the Caravelle or the Continental and take a taxi to the fighting. Or if you wanted to go farther afield you could always hitch a ride in a helicopter. Correspondents in Vietnam were given the privileges of a Major and therefore were able to command seats in most aircraft.

You could leave the hotel after breakfast and be in the middle of a firefight a couple of hours later. Sometimes you would come back dirty, tired, sickened by the slaughter and very, very frightened. You might also have little copy to send, for after a time readers become bored with just another story of bullets whistling through the palm trees and you might have acquired a much better picture of what was going on by organizing some high-powered interviews.

'Never again', you would say to yourself, 'never again.' But then you would have a shower and a drink and begin to feel better. At

Correspondents could take a taxi to the fighting

dinner somebody would come in with news of a good operation planned for the next day. 'No', you would say, 'I've had enough.' Your friends would look at you and say nothing. And then the 'firefight syndrome' would start working on you. 'Have I lost my nerve? . . . Am I burnt out? . . . Will they think I am a coward? . . .'

The fact that they knew you were not a coward did not matter. Suddenly you were having to prove to yourself that you had not lost your nerve and the next morning you would take the taxi to the war once again. 'For the last time', you would tell yourself. The trouble is that the 'firefight syndrome' not only takes you back to the war it also leads you into taking greater risks. Soldiers called up for a year's service in Vietnam used to be very careful not to get involved in anything dangerous as their tour ran out – they would paint the message 'Don't shoot, I'm short' on their helmets – but the approaching end of a correspondent's tour used to have the opposite effect with the journalist returning to the battlefield again and again, determined to get one last action story. As a result, Vietnam saw a number of correspondents killed just as they were due to go home.

It was also the place where a number of daring young men and women freelances, especially the new breed of photo-journalists, made their reputations. They arrived, often with minimal accreditation and hardly any money, and went out into the 'boondocks' with the troops. They were especially prone to the 'firefight syndrome' not only because of their own determination to succeed but also because Vietnam became essentially a war of pictures, and editors who had never been to war demanded more and more action pictures from the front line.

'Scribblers' could write stories in the safety of their hotel rooms but 'snappers' had nowhere to go except into danger.

THE PRESS AND THE MILITARY

Many of them were opposed to the war and the way it was being run, and their pictures of war at its most horrific, projected the same day into millions of homes, had a profound effect, strengthening the anti-war movement all round the world. Alas, it also had a profound effect on them. Some of the brightest and best like Sean Flynn, who used to roar around Vietnam on a motor cycle, were killed. Others, like Tim Page, were terribly wounded, others sought solace in drink and drugs. Not many correspondents escaped Vietnam untouched. They became as much victims of the war as the soldiers and villagers whose fate they described.

Their work and attitude towards authority did not appeal to the higher echelons of the US and South Vietnamese administrations, but that has always been the lot of the war correspondent. It can be argued that the correspondent who does not cause rage among officialdom is not doing his job properly. This leads me to my second maxim for would-be war correspondents: never trust officials; they are your natural enemies.

When William Russell, the first, and still one of the greatest of modern war correspondents, exposed the blunders and inadequacies of the British army in the Crimea he was accused of treason and Prince Albert called him a 'miserable scribbler'.

He was abused in London and roughly treated by young officers in the Crimea. Nevertheless, he would not succumb to the pressure and eventually his despatches helped defeat the government and brought about the reform of the army.

This first bruising encounter between the army and war correspondents established the love-hate relationship which has persisted ever since.

During the Boer War some officers thought that Winston Churchill ought to be court-martialled for revealing details of military operations in his despatches to the *Morning Post*, and the military commanders, Lord Kitchener and Lord Roberts, did their best to keep him away from the action because of his past criticisms. Eventually Churchill received a grudging message from Roberts' private secretary: 'Lord Roberts has desired me to say that he is willing to permit you to accompany this force as a correspondent – for your father's sake.' Churchill was enraged. He maintained he had every right to be with the army as a correspondent, not as a favour to his father, Lord Randolph Churchill.

Kitchener loathed war correspondents. He called them 'drunken swabs' and in the First World War did his best to stop them obtaining any news at all, ordering the arrest and expulsion from France of any correspondent found in the field. At the same time he was a great self-publicist on his own terms.

The relationship between the press and the military started equally badly in the Second World War. The arrangements made to cover the war in France in 1939 were abysmal and the Germans, with expert teams of journalists and cameramen integrated into the army, easily won the early propaganda war. They did of course have the initial advantage of being on the winning side in the shooting war.

It was not until the British government realized it could not fight a people's war without keeping the people informed that a proper system was organized with accredited correspondents covering every aspect of the fighting. Even so, they were strictly controlled and censored. They wore uniform and were subject to military law and it was not until late in the war when they had won the acceptance of the armed services that the restrictions were eased.

The Americans adopted much of the British system in the Second World War and reimposed strict censorship during the Korean War. The British followed suit in Korea and returned to a full war correspondent set-up complete with uniforms for the Suez operation.

The Americans were unable to do this in Vietnam, however, because they were not officially at war. They were simply 'assisting' the South Vietnamese resist aggression; therefore they could not impose censorship or restrict travel.

The result was that while the North Vietnamese strictly controlled their propaganda machine the Americans were faced by free-wheeling, often hostile, reportage which many embittered government officials and generals remain convinced cost the USA the war.

It was fear of Vietnam-type reporting and its supposed affect on the will of the people to maintain the struggle – 'wait till the body-bags start coming home' – that led to the imposition of severe restrictions on the reporting of the Falklands Conflict and the Gulf War.

Any news of importance in the Falklands fighting was issued by the Ministry of Defence and the correspondents' copy was doubly censored, in the Falklands and in London. In the Gulf War only those reporters in the official 'pools' got any assistance from the allied authorities and they were strictly limited in what they could see, do, and report. The so-called 'unilaterals' were given no help whatsoever and were harried and chivvied by the authorities for being outside their restricted areas. Some were arrested and threatened with expulsion. It was Kitchener all over again. Many of them, however, simply got into their cars and took off into the desert, avoiding both the mines and the 'minders' to get on-the-spot stories often denied to the 'pool' correspondents.

GOING PREPARED

Given the danger from shot and shell, from the stress caused by seeing the effects of war and from the constant battle with authority in its various forms I can quite understand the bemusement of the young US soldier in a particularly unpleasant place in Vietnam who said to me: 'What bugs me about you guys is that you don't have to be here if you don't want to.'

He was probably right, but suppose, for one reason or another, you are determined to be a war correspondent, how do you go about it as a freelance?

First of all remember the maxims: a dead correspondent is a bad correspondent and a good correspondent is bound to have trouble with the authorities.

The next thing to do is to make sure that you are properly prepared. When a staff correspondent is sent to a war zone he or she will have the resources of a large organization as back-up. You will have nothing and so you must prepare yourself carefully for your assignment. If you know nothing about the area where your chosen war is taking place, go to the library, read the back numbers of the papers, get out your cuttings, consult the encyclopaedias, buy some tourist guide books, get a decent map, study the history of the conflict and the personalities of the generals involved and organize a briefing from an expert. It also pays to acquire some knowledge of the weaponry being used. Now you will at least have some sort of background for your stories.

You should make sure you are in reasonable physical shape. I do not suggest for one moment that you should take a crash course at a gym – that usually does more harm than good – but there is absolutely no point in going into a hostile environment if you are sick or cannot walk a few miles without collapsing. To walk into the Afghan hills with the mujahideen was an ordeal for the fittest person even before they got within sound of the fighting.

You will have had the necessary jabs for the area in which you propose to work. Although Africa and Asia are only a few hours' flight away from your own environment they remain the breeding grounds of the most appalling diseases. Do not take risks: Malaria, Hepatitis, Polio, Yellow Fever, Cholera are all preventable with the right jabs and drugs although one form or another of the dreaded stomach bug is inevitable. Aids is the latest deadly disease lying in wait for the unwary and the only thing you can do about this is *don't*.

It is sensible to carry a small medicine box with you. The BBC issues a medical kit to all its staff in the field. Alas, when John Simpson was stung by a huge hornet in Iraq his kit lacked the anti-hystamine ointment needed to treat the bite. His leg came up 'like a marrow' and he had to make an eighteen-hour journey to Turkey for treatment. What you take depends on where you are going and your own susceptibilities. My own basic medical kit consists of a bandage, plasters, antiseptic and anti-hystamine ointments, mosquito repellent, Vaseline, indigestion tablets, lomotil or something similar for the inevitable stomach bug, aspirin, pain-killing tablets, tablets for sore throats and coughs, scissors, sharp knife or razor blade and tweezers. All this should fit into a washbag.

STRESS AND GLORY

Having made your physical preparations you must also prepare yourself mentally. It is not possible to be inoculated against the horrors of war but you can read about battle and talk to people who have experienced it so that you have some idea of what you are getting yourself into.

When you become a war correspondent, you will probably see more action than most soldiers simply because it is your job to travel the world in search of action while many regular soldiers go through a lifetime of service without hearing a shot fired in anger, and, indeed, without wishing to do so.

Today, if a soldier goes into action people are prepared for him to suffer from post-battle stress but for some strange reason correspondents are presumed to be impervious to the horrors of the battlefield.

You will find out that this is not so. You will see things too awful to write about but which will stick in your mind forever. You can hide them away, pen them up, but they will take you by surprise and come rushing out, triggered by some random event: a chance remark at a dinner table, a television programme, a photograph. The pity of it is that the best war correspondents are usually the most sensitive and therefore suffer the most.

The people who really ought not to be war correspondents are the 'cowboys' who glory in the superficialities of war. They never understand that they are a danger to themselves and to their colleagues. So, if you aspire to be 'Rambo' please do not attempt to become a war correspondent.

During the 1973 war in the Middle East I found myself with a group of correspondents in a bus organized by the Israelis to take us to the scene of a battle. One young man left the bus, wandered around the desert oblivious to the danger of mines and unexploded shells, and searched for souvenirs, and was upset when the Israelis told him he would not be allowed back on the bus with the loaded AK 47 he had picked up. Then, as we drove back, some of us sipped a contemplative whisky from a hipflask prudently carried by a veteran in these affairs. Wanting to copy the big boys, our young man stopped the bus as we passed through an Arab village and bought a bottle of arak which he proceeded to swig. After a few miles, he vomited all over the bus. It emerged he was the editor of a small college newspaper and had never been out of his home state before. The Israelis had accredited him as a correspondent because they needed all the sympathy they could get in the USA.

CREDENTIALS

So, you have made your preparations, you are in the right frame of mind and you are eager to go; but who is going to send you to your war? You may be able to finance yourself in the sure expectation that you are going to make your reputation and your fortune, but in this field more than in any other you need letters of accreditation, preferably on thick notepaper with a fine embossed letterhead and several impressive stamps. Before allowing correspondents to join the party most countries need to be assured that somebody is responsible for them and for any debts they might run up, so the more impressive the letter of accreditation the more effect it has.

Officials are also impressed by faxes and if you can persuade whoever has given you the assignment to send a flurry of faxes announcing your impending arrival so much the better. It also pays to get letters of accreditation from a number of clients so that if a letter disappears into the local bureaucracy, or you become unpopular as the representative of that particular newspaper, you can reappear in a new untarnished guise.

CARRYING MONEY

You should also organize your finances before setting out. In the old days the intrepid correspondent in the Middle East would have a supply of Maria Theresa dollars sewn into the lining of his jacket. These days it is wiser not to have all your financial eggs in one jacket.

It is best to be equipped with currency, travellers' cheques and credit cards. You have to be careful with local currency, however. Many countries forbid the import of their own currency on the usually justifiable grounds that it has been bought at a much cheaper rate than the official bank rate. These are the countries where dealers will offer very good rates for foreign currency and travellers' cheques, but be careful; their activities are usually illegal and you need to be sure you can trust them before you enter into transactions.

However, the official exchange rates are often set at such a ridiculous rate that you have no alternative but to use the black market, or pay for everything by credit card. You will find that the US dollar is the foreign currency most accepted. Travellers' cheques and credit cards are both useful because they mean that you do not have to carry large amounts of cash and are replaceable as long as you can get a telephone call through to the issuing company or bank. Make sure that your assets are split up among your pockets and baggage so that if one lot is stolen you have not lost everything. Never, never, flash a large wad of notes around. It is an invitation to a mugging.

Sometimes you can be too clever. One journalist I know covering the war between Somalia and Ethiopia put a large bundle of money he was carrying into a hole in the wall behind a light fitting and it fell down the cavity behind the plaster. He had to break down the wall to get his money back – and pay for the damage.

Finally, if you are in a Third World country, always spend or convert your local currency before you leave. If you don't it will probably be confiscated at the airport where the bureau de change is conveniently shut. If you do manage to get it out you will find that its value has plummeted. I have a drawer at home full of useless bits of exotic currencies.

TRAVELLING TO WAR

Having made your preparations for going to war you will still be faced with one major problem: how to get there. The first thing that happens when fighting breaks out is that the airports are closed and you are immediately denied that favourite opening sentence: 'I flew into wartorn Utopia today . . .' You must then decide whether to sweat it out at the nearest open airport, gambling that the air service will soon reopen, or make arrangements to go in by other means.

When the Vietcong made Saigon's Tan Son Nhut airport too dangerous for civilian traffic during the Tet offensive in 1968, correspondents flew to Bangkok. There, on the far side of the glossy international airport, the Americans had set up a mini airbase. After masses of 'documentation' we were confronted by a medical orderly who insisted on plunging a huge hypodermic into every correspondent. He said it was to prevent us catching the plague but we were convinced he was a sadist.

We then waited around until dark when we were loaded on an ancient Dakota along with a group of hard-faced men in civilian clothes who refused to say a word to the correspondents. Saigon was easy to see. Flames from burning buildings licked the night sky, smoke drifted across the moon, you could see the fiery tails of rockets as they roared out of the jungle to explode in the city and the answering muzzle flashes of the US cannon as they sought out the Vietcong rocketeers.

We got down safely, manhandled the plane into a sandbagged revetment and spent the rest of the night under the wing pinned down by fire from both directions.

That was one way of getting to a war. Another way had to be found when Beirut erupted and the airport was put out of action. Correspondents who had gathered in Cyprus as the nearest neutral ante-room to the war were eventually accommodated by a daring skipper who took them on his ferry, running the gauntlet of Moslem shellfire, to a port held by the Christian militia north of Beirut.

Often it is simpler to hire a car or a trusted taxi-driver and drive to a little used crossing point on the border and hope to slip, or bribe your way, across. If you choose to do this take plenty of cigarettes. You may not smoke but most border guards do.

This method has its dangers simply because of its uncertainties. You never know what sort of reception you are going to get. An unfriendly tank may appear round the corner at any time and the local secret policemen may take exception to you. You could get kidnapped.

It is best therefore if you travel as a party with other correspondents. One man or woman on their own are easy game, but nothing is more frightening than a dozen newspaper correspondents from different countries, all waving bits of paper with official looking stamps and shouting in strange languages.

This may seem the antithesis of the romantic image of the war-correspondent loner but it is much, much safer. Even when you have got to the war it is better to work out some sort of alliance with a small group of correspondents who are not in competition with you. Covering a war is a demanding, exhausting business. Not only are you in some physical danger, you have to acquire your story, write it and get it out. You also have to make sure there is fuel in the car, that you have somewhere to sleep and food to eat. You have to make contact with the army and the civil authorities. With others to share the burden of these tasks and to watch your back, life becomes easier and there is no disgrace in sharing a story with, for example, someone from a French or German or African newspaper – it will also help build up your freelance contacts.

GOING IT ALONE

If, however, you do decide to go it alone, you must be careful. Suppose the border is closed and the only way across is on foot along some sheeptrack. You are vulnerable from the moment you set out. You will need a guide, but can the person be trusted? Will they betray you or rob you? You will not know until it happens or they deliver you safely. The only thing you can do is to cut the odds. Do not flash large wads of money. Agree a fee in front of witnesses. Pay only part of it before you set out. Make sure your guide knows that you have written an account of your arrangement naming him and have given it to someone in case anything goes wrong.

Having taken your precautions, keep your side of the bargain without demur. Never, ever, do anything by look, word or action that could be construed as an insult to local womanhood and if you should be a woman or have a woman with you make sure that no offence is given to local customs by dress or behaviour. Nothing arouses an Afghan tribesman to religious and/or sexual fervour quicker than a western woman behaving immodestly.

All this may seem to be basic common-sense but the type who sets out on this sort of adventure usually has the adrenalin flowing and common sense comes a long way down the list of priorities. The danger is that getting across the border becomes an all-important end in itself whereas in reality it is only a means of getting to the story.

You never get much sympathy from editors if you put yourself at risk, slogging across some mountain pass in the company of some villainous goatherd who is charging you a fortune for leading you along a path he uses every day only to find that you have been beaten to the story because the airport has been opened and your rivals who have been lazing around a hotel swimming pool have flown in and had a pleasant dinner with the embassy's defence attache.

The murder in 1991 of Nick della Casa and Charles Maxwell and the abduction and probable murder of Nick's wife, Rosanna, while crossing from Turkey into Iraq to cover the Kurdish uprising for the BBC is a tragic example of the dangers run by adventurous journalists.

SENDING COPY

Let us suppose that, by one means or another, you have arrived safely at the war. If it is a proper war then, undoubtedly, the local authorities will wish to have some control of your movements and what you write. If they are organized it is difficult to avoid this control so it is often better to accept it and make use of it. Pick the most powerful men, ask to interview them, flatter them, make friends with them. Get their names on *laissez-passers* so that when you get to the front you are properly escorted and treated with respect.

It is now that the arrangements you have made to market your copy have their effect on your operations. If you are committed to a long-term article for a magazine then there is no reason why you should not go up to the front and stay with the soldiers. You are in Kipling and Hemingway territory now and soldiers under fire always make good copy. This is undoubtedly the sort of reporting most war correspondents prefer.

It maybe, however, that your brief is not to disappear into the 'boonies' but to provide a daily service of news. In which case you cannot afford to spend a long time at the front. You must not outrun your communications and there may be more important stories breaking in the capital than in the trenches. Even if you are writing once a week for a Sunday you will have to split your time between the politicians and the soldiers to provide a rounded picture of the conflict.

Moreover, as a freelance in a war zone you will be able to use the capital's facilities to sell your copy around the world once you have satisfied your contracted clients' needs – which is difficult to do if you are sitting in a bunker under fire without any communications.

It is one of the ironies of journalism that some correspondents gain a bigger reputation and a fatter bank balance by making a few telephone calls from the poolside of the local Hilton than by actually going to the war. They do not, however, gain the respect of their colleagues.

BRIEFINGS AND DISINFORMATION

Actually writing about war may seem simple, if occasionally dangerous. The story, it is said, 'writes itself'. It is not that simple, however, for the good war correspondent to write about the politics of war as well as the crash-bang and he must tread a very careful line, trying to tell the truth without enraging the people for whom the war is a matter of life and death rather than column inches and elegant writing.

Undoubtedly they will try to influence what the correspondent writes in order to present their country in a good light and to help win the war. Disinformation – lies and half lies – is the stock in trade of information officers. Sometimes the lies become so outrageous that the propaganda machine loses all credence.

The notorious 'Four O'Clock Follies', the daily briefing given by the Americans in Saigon, was so 'sanitized' that correspondents returning from the front could hardly believe that the smartly dressed officers were talking about the same firefight in which they had just been involved. In the end these briefings did positive harm to the US and South Vietnamese cause because nobody believed the briefing officers even when they told the truth.

The important thing is not to accept implicitly what you are told. Ask questions. Ferret around. Talk to the ordinary soldiers, they may have only a limited view of the overall picture but they can certainly smell out disinformation.

This will make you unpopular with the authorities and pressure will be applied, either to your editor or personally with the removal of facilities and the threat of expulsion. The trick is to write the story so that you get your message across without getting yourself kicked out – unless you want to.

PROPAGANDA AND TRUTH

You may, of course, become so committed to one side in a war that you believe everything the propagandists tell you and you become a propagandist yourself. It is very easy if you spend time with troops under fire to identify with them and begin to think in terms of 'us' and 'them'. This certainly happened in the Middle East during the Six Day War when many correspondents identified with the Israelis although this was partly the fault of the Arab nations who barred all foreign war correspondents.

It works the other way as well. Some correspondents became so opposed to US involvement in Vietnam that while disbelieving everything the Americans said, they swallowed North Vietnamese propaganda without a murmur.

There are also correspondents who are politically committed to one side of a cause and they cover their wars from their political viewpoint. In extreme cases their journalism becomes only a tool to spread their political views. The Spanish Civil War was perhaps the most extreme example of a war in which the correspondents on both sides were politicized, some of them, like Claude Cockburn and Arthur Koestler, to the extent of fabricating stories, concocting fiction not for the headlines but for the good of the political cause. Kim Philby, reporting the war for *The Times*, added another twist by writing approving stories from the Franco camp while actually working for the Soviet secret service.

It is, of course, impossible to keep one's feelings out of one's copy while writing about something as elemental and emotional as war but if you aspire to be a journalist rather than a polemicist it is both wiser and more honest to try to tell the story straight. The facts of war are strong enough to speak for themselves. They do not need embellishment or bias; and they should not be used selectively to support the writer's views.

The truth is too difficult to obtain, especially in war time, for reporters to taint it with their own propaganda. You have an obligation to your readers to tell it as it is, and, not as you would wish it to be.

This is, moreover, a question not only of journalistic honesty but of self-preservation for if you write lies for the big headlines or the political cause you will eventually be found out, and life gets hard for a discredited freelance correspondent. Suddenly, nobody invites you to the war any more.

Sometimes a war develops which, by its nature, is virtually impossible for freelances to cover in their usual cavalier style. Bosnia is a good but bloody example. Up till the end of 1993 nearly forty journalists died covering the fighting between the Serbs, Croats and Moslems. Civil wars are always the most dangerous to cover because of the fragmented nature of the battlefield and the ill-disciplined behaviour of partisan groups. This is especially so when, as in Bosnia, it is a three-way war because you never know where the danger is coming from. But never before have journalists been deliberately targeted, murdered in order to force them out of areas so that atrocities could be committed in secrecy. By the late spring of 1992 journalists – and aid workers – had been driven from most of Bosnia outside the main towns so that the cruelties of 'ethnic cleansing' could be carried out unreported.

The physical danger in Bosnia is the same for all journalists but freelances find it especially difficult to continue covering the war because of the added costs and limitations imposed by the dangers.

There is no question of adopting the normal war correspondent's technique of taking a taxi to the fighting. In Bosnia it has to be a well-armoured car, hired or bought at enormous cost.

Steel helmets and flak jackets are not just for posing in but are *de rigueur* for safety and they, too, have to be bought or hired. Personal insurance premiums are sky-high – if any company can be found brave enough to gamble on the journalist staying alive. Accommodation and food outside the UN messes is scarce and expensive. In Sarajevo most journalists stay at the Holiday Hotel but like everywhere else in that once charming town, it is subject to water and electricity cuts and the food is basic. Those correspondents employed by the major news organizations have essential supplies, especially bottled water, flown in. Clothing is also an expensive problem; winter in an unheated Sarajevo demands special cold weather clothing and any expedition into the snow-covered hills entails dressing for arctic warfare.

All this expense can be borne by the television companies and newspapers – although their accounts departments will moan – but they are insupportable for the average freelance. It might be different if the freelances were confident of earning a lot of money from their enterprise and skill but the difficulties of covering the war negate all but the most exceptional enterprise, skill – and luck.

To get to Sarajevo, all correspondents need a UN visa and when they are flown in on a UN supply aircraft they find that they are involved in pool arrangements for covering stories.

Any travel they may do depends on the hospitality of the UN forces, or by begging lifts from staff correspondents with armoured cars and chancing the uncertain, usually drunken, cooperation of militiamen at the road blocks. This is hardly conducive to winning fame as a freelance war correspondent which requires a certain freedom of action and the ability to seek out stories not covered by the big battalions of the staffers.

Some freelances have, however, flourished in Bosnia by selling their services on a contractual basis to newspapers and television to replace staff correspondents who, for various reasons, are deployed elsewhere; there aren't too many staffers who actually enjoy Bosnia. In this way the freelances have acquired regular incomes and the all-important logistical back-up of powerful organizations. Those that have succeeded have also gained the professional respect of the exclusive war correspondents' club and the experience to survive and succeed in other wars.

One man, at least, has made a great success of such an

arrangement. Tony Birtley, a freelance working for ITN in Bosnia, was named television journalist of the year in the Royal Television Society's journalism awards in February 1994.

The lessons to be learnt from Bosnia are that freelance war correspondents must choose their wars carefully, must ensure they have enough contracted work and back-up to make it worthwhile, must understand that journalists can become deliberate rather than accidental targets and that when a war becomes too difficult to cover the best policy is to take off for greener and safer pastures.

I have just one more maxim for the would-be war correspondent. You will hear it said like a mantra as reporters leave for the front line: 'Keep your head down'.

9 SPECIALIST AREAS: TERRORISM

Writing about terrorism is a specialized branch of war reporting, and, indeed, a good example of a freelance specialism. Sometimes, as in Vietnam, when terrorism develops into guerrilla warfare and then into full-scale war, the one form of reporting merges with the other, but curiously while many young reporters want to be war correspondents, few looking for a specialism would want to become experts on terrorism.

I say curiously because it is a rich specialist field with a constant flow of stories. Perhaps journalists shy away from it because it is so complicated, requiring a talent for appreciating the finer points of intrigue rather than the broad sweep of conventional warfare.

One needs to know, for example, the difference between the PFLP – General Command and the PFLP – Special Command, rival offshoots of the original Popular Front for the Liberation of Palestine, and why members of the Irish National Liberation Army kill one another in outbursts of bloody internecine murder. It is also necessary to understand the history, politics and social conditions of the countries in which the various groups operate and what leads certain states to sponsor terrorism.

All this takes much study, travel and interviewing. There are easier ways for staff journalists to make their names and many newspapers have no specialists in this field at all so that when a terrorist story breaks, newsdesks start a frantic search to find someone who can quickly put together some words which are expert, which can explain what has happened, but which can still be understood by the ordinary person.

The terrorist field, therefore, is wide open to the freelance who cares to specialize in it.

BACKGROUND MATERIAL

The first thing to realize is that there is an extensive pool of knowledge on this subject, not only in the cuttings dealing with incidents, but in books and papers written by academics and military experts. It was journalists who first started writing about terrorism with the advent of 'Black September' and 'spectaculars' like the massacre of the Israeli athletes at the Munich Olympics in 1972. At first the academics rather scorned terrorism as a passing phase, a 'blip' in international relations, but they soon realized it was here to stay and saw the advantages of specializing in its study. Universities set up departments and appointed professors to study this new field of learning.

The irony of this situation was that the academics were at first almost entirely dependent on the facts gathered by journalists who covered the terrorist outrages and who interviewed the groups' leaders. Armed with this information, the academics brought their training in research to bear and rapidly became sought after as consultants to businesses, governments and the anti-terrorist forces.

The result has been an outpouring of books on the various terrorist organizations, on the morality of terrorism, the politics of terrorism, the weapons of terrorism, the organization of the anti-terrorist forces, every aspect of the subject; the military authors have contributed their specialized knowledge and so a good grounding in the subject is available on the library shelves and, because the subject is only a couple of decades old, almost all of them are relevant.

There are also some excellent publications issued by interested organizations like the US State Department whose annual *Patterns of Global Terrorism* is an essential work of reference. The Rand Institute in California also publishes papers full of invaluable information. Professor Paul Wilkinson, director of the Institute for the Study of Conflict and Terrorism and the leading academic in this field in the UK, produces work of the highest order. His report on the Lockerbie bombing is a model of analytical research. Tel Aviv University is particularly good on the intricacies of the Arab groups and the Jonathan Institute, named after 'Yoni' Netanyahu, killed leading the assault at Entebbe, is dedicated to educating the public about terrorism.

The strengths of these institutions lie in the fact that they are well-funded, can afford trained researchers and have large computers whose databanks are filled with information.

No journalist could acquire such information alone, but these institutions are in the business of disseminating information and once you have broken into the network you will find yourself acquiring a basic library and, more important, the telephone numbers of the people who can answer your questions.

The beauty of having such a store of knowledge at your disposal is that when an act of terrorism takes place you do not need more than a couple of paragraphs of news to build a comprehensive story. You will have the background in your files or, at least, at the end of the telephone.

DISKS AND INDEXING

I record the details of every important act of terrorism on a disk – a card index will do just as well – and a quick search through the files reveals dates and names and places and methods involved in the incidents. From this information I can build up a picture of similar incidents, tracing trends, organizations and methods. At the cost of a few minutes' filing I have an invaluable journalistic tool literally at my fingertips.

Let us take, for example, the IRA mortar attack on 10 Downing Street during the Gulf War. Because of the threats by Palestinian terror groups to carry the war to the West on behalf of Saddam Hussein some editors jumped to the conclusion that the origins of this attack lay in the Middle East.

It was immediately obvious from the file, however, that the IRA was almost certainly responsible because the method of attack and the weapons involved had been developed and used on a number of occasions by the IRA and had never been used by the Palestinians. It broke my heart to turn down a profitable commission to write a story saying that Saddam Hussein had struck at the heart of London but I am glad that I did for within a few hours it was firmly established that the IRA was responsible. I had made the right, if unprofitable, decision because a study of the file left me with no alternative.

The value of such files applies not only to terrorism but to all other journalistic specializations. I cannot stress too strongly the importance of keeping all the information you gather in an orderly and accessible system.

BEING ON THE SPOT

One way in which the journalist still has the advantage over the academic is in the ability to gather information on the spot. At the height of the troubles in Beirut the Palestinian organizations still had their numbers listed in the telephone book and it was possible to arrange interviews with some of the world's most feared terrorists. It is these interviews and on-the-spot reportage of incidents which flesh out the analysis of the academics. For example, I found my description of the interior of the Fatah headquarters in Beirut appearing in books published all over the world.

The lesson here is to write down, on such occasions, an absolutely detailed description: the posters on the walls, the weapons stacked against the wall, the bits and pieces on the desk. Type out the conversation. Everything will be of use one day.

I once spent an afternoon with Bassam Abu Sherif, then spokesman for the Popular Front for the Liberation of Palestine, in his office in Beirut. He had recently been terribly wounded by an Israeli parcel-bomb and was bitterly extreme in his views. He railed against the 'imperialist West' and swore that Israel would be destroyed. His office was littered with the debris of terrorist wars and there were quotations from Irish revolutionaries on the wall. Some years later he became a moderate and was appointed political adviser to Yasser Arafat. Wearing a smart suit and oozing charm and diplomacy, he came to London to negotiate with the Foreign Office on behalf of the PLO. Few people in London knew anything about him so my notes of our meeting provided the basis for a number of background stories.

TERRORISTS AND THE PRESS

This brings us to the question of how you deal with terrorists. These are serious men and, while the terrorist logic with which they justify themselves may seem unreal, they must be treated seriously. The journalistic problem is how to report what they have to say without becoming a vehicle for their propaganda or falling victim to disinformation – or antagonizing them.

The IRA's sophisticated propaganda machine was so successful in getting its propaganda displayed – if not believed – on British television that the government banned members of the IRA and Sinn Fein from the screen on the grounds that murderers should not be given access to television to justify their horrendous deeds.

One of the IRA propaganda coups which enraged the authorities took place in 1979 when a force of armed IRA men armed with heavy machine guns, rocket propelled grenades and Armalite rifles sealed off the village of Carrickmore for more than three hours as a stunt for a BBC Panorama film team. News of the exercise leaked out and the programme was banned.

The ban on allowing IRA members to speak on television in order to deny them 'the oxygen of publicity' caused an outcry about freedom of the press and some television companies have got round the ban by getting actors to voice-over the terrorists' banned words. The BBC, interviewing IRA prisoners in the Maze jail adopted another ploy, arguing that they were speaking in a 'personal capacity' and not as representatives of the IRA or Sinn Fein.

This is a delicate area for journalists because, apart from the committed few who support the IRA cause, nobody wants to help murderers, but at the same time the idea of relinquishing the hard-won right to print what one likes within the bounds of decency and libel is anathema to all journalists. It is especially delicate for freelances, for while staff correspondents follow the line of conduct laid down by their newspapers and can absolve themselves by pleading *force majeure*, freelances have only their own common sense and code of conduct to guide their actions.

Nothing is simple where the IRA is concerned. Once a freelance arrives in Ireland to cover the troubles the rival propaganda machines of the security forces and the IRA start a battle for his or her soul and pen. The IRA feeds the freelance stories about the brutality of the British army, and the army press officers spread rumours like the famous story designed to sap the IRA's morale that the handling of plastic explosives causes leukemia. Nowhere in the world are correspondents deluged with such a mass of disinformation as in Belfast.

Some journalists have found themselves on the IRA hit list and others have been warned that their presence is no longer welcome in Belfast.

On the other hand the authorities can take action against reporters who are thought to be too close to the IRA cause. Nothing drastic, of course; just a quiet word here and another there and suddenly the commissions dry up.

So Ireland is a dangerous place but, if you want to specialize in terrorism, you have to go there. You have to walk down the Falls Road, you have to visit Crossmaglen and the Bogside in Londonderry, talk to the Unionists and the Nationalists, go out on patrol with the Army and see how the RUC tries to police the province.

Until you catch the smell of fear and resentment, listen to the old grievances and sympathize with the people trying to lead ordinary lives in the world of the bomb and the bullet you will not be able to write about terrorism.

One of the things that makes this subject such a demanding but at the same time rewarding one to cover is that it is always changing, always developing. New alliances are formed, new enemies are made, new weapons and tactics are adopted.

SOURCES AND BENEFITS

A bomb scoring an 'own goal', an abortive operation or a police swoop can mean the sudden and violent end of some of your contacts. The same thing applies to the security services. Just when you think you have your sources properly organized, a posting or a death can ruin your contact.

New methods, new equipment are introduced. New laws are passed, new advances made in the technical aspects of the prevention of terrorism. If you are going to cover the subject properly, you must keep up with all the technical and political developments, attend symposiums, renew your contacts – and keep and update your files.

As with other specialisms or sought-after subjects – espionage, for example – once you have established yourself as an expert you may find that the benefits will come not only from writing newspaper stories but also from appearing on radio and television and maybe even consultancy work, lectures and after-dinner speeches. These are the things that can help you enjoy the greatest of the joys of being a freelance: independence.

10 MAGAZINES AND SUPPLEMENTS

Freelances who opt for more peaceable ways of pursuing their profession than those described in the last three chapters might become involved in magazine work. The advantage of such work is that there is an enormous number of magazines, they eat up a vast amount of copy and they usually have a small permanent staff and so have to rely on freelances for their material.

At the top end of the market are those magazines like *Reader's Digest* and the *National Geographic* which have huge international circulations. They work to rigid formulas and their editors are exceedingly difficult to satisfy. The *Reader's Digest* in particular puts a contributor's copy through a most rigid examination for accuracy; you cannot get away with any sloppiness in your writing. On the other hand, these magazines pay handsomely. It should also be remembered that the *Reader's Digest* runs its own book publishing section for which it requires a great deal of freelance work. The rewards are not as great when working for this section as they are when working for the magazine itself, but there is more work available.

The weekend supplements of the national newspapers are also great eaters of material. Until recently the Saturday editions were looked on by managements as a bit of a nuisance to print, fit only for late-breaking news – usually of a disaster – and page after page of sport. Now the money men are looking at Saturday papers as part of a profitable weekend package and they have become almost as fat as the Sunday papers.

This means that the freelance has a range of supplements to aim at in addition to the traditional glossy Sunday magazines. *The Times Saturday Review* has some 50 pages of features, travel, reviews, fashion, cooking, and contains all those regular specialist features such as chess, bridge and crosswords which develop a devoted following among readers. It is in fact a complete magazine, as is the comparable *Daily Telegraph Weekend* and similar supplements given away by most of the national and many provincial newspapers.

The point is that they are filled with mainly freelance copy and what has been created is a whole new source of income for freelances.

Another major source of magazine income for freelances is women's magazines. You have only to look at the serried ranks of these publications on the railway station bookstalls to realize what a rich and competitive market this is. The giants of the industry like IPC which publishes scores of magazines, use production line techniques with very small staffs. This means that they rely on freelance writers and sub-editors to fill and handle the pages. One of the advantages of becoming accepted by the large publishing houses is that while they do not pay over-generously, there are so many magazines published from the same building that it is easy for a freelance to make contacts and to work for more than one magazine at the same time.

The grapevine in such organizations rapidly spreads your name among the editors as a person worth using or, on the other hand, as a trouble maker not to be allowed anywhere near the office.

While the staffs of women's magazines are mostly women there is no bar to copy written by men. There is a strong element of show business, especially television, in many of them and that can be written by a man just as well as a woman. It must be pointed out, however, that because they are essentially magazines run for women by women, the problems of women contributors are better understood. So a woman freelance, struggling to raise a family as well as pursue her career, might usefully gravitate to working for a women's magazine.

USING EXPERTISE

If you are an expert in a certain subject and can write it does not matter if you are male or female. What does matter is that the more esoteric your subject the fewer outlets you have. Almost every magazine has a health column or a gardening corner but not many, for example, carry stories on the mysteries of the computer. You have to turn to the specialized publications to be given hints on how to write a software programme. What a freelance has to decide is if writing for such specialized magazines is going to pay enough. The answer in most cases is no.

The specialist magazines are designed to be profitable by filling a certain hole in the market. That means a fixed circulation and a tight budget. Nobody is going to make a fortune out of them except the publishers. You might have fun writing for them but you will not grow rich.

GRAFTING AND TARGETING

So, how do we go about writing for magazines? We have to tap the source. There is no easy way. Well-known writers and former staff members of the parent newspapers of supplements have an obvious advantage because their work is known and trusted but if you are just starting out, you have to peddle your wares until you too become well-known and trusted and the commissioning editor calls you instead of you calling him.

If is hard graft and often dispiriting as you hawk your ideas from office to office, but if you are going to make the grade as a freelance you have to do it. Pick your targets. Be persistent without making a nuisance of yourself. Keep up a bombardment of ideas; editors will crack eventually. Take the commissioning editor out to lunch. The bill may make you wince but it puts your guest under an obligation and if you can charm either him or her, so much the better. Use your contacts ruthlessly but with style.

This advice presupposes that when you are eventually given an assignment you will be able to deliver the words that are wanted because if you cannot do the business you would be much better off forgetting about freelancing. You will not survive.

CHOOSING SUBJECTS

There is also the question of what you intend to write about. There are certain subjects which have such a universal appeal that they command space in almost any general magazine. Show business, royalty, sex, health, wealth, crime and sport top the list.

Readers are thought to have an insatiable urge to know everything about the people they see on their television screens. An interview with a TV 'personality' is almost certain to make a sale. Stories about forthcoming attractions and the actors who will star in them are snapped up; gossip, especially about the love lives of the stars, finds a ready home in the tabloids; and once a show becomes a success everybody associated with it including long-dead authors become newsworthy. Whoever would have thought that H.E. Bates would become a household name? The 'Darling Buds of May' made him one. And who would have thought that a tubby Italian opera singer would become an idol to masses of English men and women who have never been to an opera? But by singing 'Nessum Dorma' from *Turandot* which was played over and over again as the theme music for the 1990 World Cup competition, Luciano Pavarotti became a pop super-star. It enraged the opera lovers of Italy but placed Pavarotti in the ranks of those who are guaranteed media-fodder.

The beauty of this situation is that everyone connives at it. The press agents of the performers, the publicity departments of the television companies, the editors of the magazines and newspapers all work together to set up interviews, disseminate stories and put them into print. It is a profitable conspiracy which the freelance has to join and become the agent who carries out the plot.

SHOWBIZ WRITING

Homegrown television has largely taken the place of Hollywood but the lives and loves of the superstars still make excellent magazine material. These stories are at their most potent and profitable when the stars have a new film which is about to be released and they appear on the TV chat shows to publicize it. The trick, as in all journalism, is getting the timing right. Magazines have a lead time of up to six weeks so it is pointless trying to sell an interview on the opening night which would not appear until six weeks later by which time everyone will have become bored with the star and the film and moved on to the next sensation. Get your interview six weeks beforehand so it can be published to coincide with the grand opening of the film or television series and you will make a certain sale.

It is said that certain stars are difficult to interview. Maybe so, but is remarkable how readily they will make themselves available if they think it will bring queues to the box office or will sell more copies of their autobiographies.

GHOST WRITING

A thought worth remembering, too, is that if you become a successful show-biz reporter you might well be asked to ghost one of those 'autobiographies'. Ghosting is an honourable if frustrating aspect of the profession. Occasionally you have to stay silent when your wittiest phrases are trotted out as the words and wisdom of some modestly educated bimbo but very often you will find your alter ego no mean performer with words and all you will need to do is to provide the professional polish.

All this may sound cynical. I do not intend it to. I am simply pointing out that show business people quite legitimately use journalists to promote themselves and there is no reason why journalists, especially freelances, should not get a slice of the action.

ROYAL STORIES

Those journalists who specialize in writing about royalty are, at first sight, faced with a completely opposite state of affairs: they are writing about people who do not want publicity, who employ press officers to keep them out of the newspapers rather than in. This is not, however, an accurate assessment of the situation for the Royal Family does need publicity and has no qualms about using it to promote its own, albeit worthy, interests.

The Queen herself promotes Great Britain through the publicity engendered by State occasions; Prince Philip raises support for the World Wide Fund for Nature; Princess Anne does sterling, eminently reportable work for the Save the Children Fund; Princess Diana is the source of excellent copy on the plight of Aids victims and the Prince of Wales commands nationwide interest for his various projects. Journalists who cooperate with the Royal Family and give publicity to their favourite causes can expect help from the Buckingham Palace Press Office and, when trusted, from the family itself.

Serious writers about the monarchy are helped by the librarian of the royal archives at Windsor and if their work is appreciated word seeps out from Buck House that members of the family and courtiers may give guarded assistance.

The point is that the Royal Family and its advisers know very well that the monarchy is a form of show business and that its success, even its survival, depends on its popularity with the people. With the days of the divine rights of kings long gone, it is their star rating which matters and they must have the 'oxygen of publicity'.

Where they differ from the other branches of show business is that whereas a film star can say 'I don't care what you write about me as long as you spell my name correctly', the Royal Family cannot bear bad publicity.

Millions of people leading very ordinary lives look to the monarchy to provide a fairy tale, a Prince and Princess Charming, to lighten their humdrum existence. They read everything written about royalty. It is a general rule of publishing that a magazine with a royal cover sells well and one with a Princess Diana cover sells out.

One of the great ironies is that those three great republics, France and Russia, which murdered their monarchs, and the USA, which gained its independence by defeating George III's army, should be so passionately interested in the British royals.

At the first British book fair in Moscow before the fall of communism the authorities did their usual trick of bussing in a group of trusted workers to demonstrate that anyone was allowed to go to foreign exhibitions. The ploy backfired, however, when all the workers gathered in front of one particular exhibit. It was a photographic album of the British Royal Family and the workers, ignoring their minders, were animatedly discussing the family resemblance between King Edward VII and their own murdered Tsar. They were quickly ushered back on to their buses.

US interest is even more paradoxical for while the idea of the British Empire remains anathema to most US citizens the Royal Family itself is held in much esteem – except by those of nationalist Irish descent – and the doings of the family, especially its younger members, excite much interest among magazine readers.

The French get even more excited, so much so that their royal coverage is often fiction with their writers churning out stories about the Queen and her children so wild that even the British tabloids do not dare to reprint them. The Queen is about to divorce Prince Philip. She is suffering from a fatal disease. And so they go on.

With such universal interest there is obviously much scope for freelancers in the royal field, and just as obviously it is a crowded field.

Most of Britain's national newspapers maintain specialists whose job is to write solely about the Royal Family. When it is hunting together this 'royal ratpack' is formidable, spending large sums of money to get the required picture or story. Individual members will fight tooth, nail and bribe to scoop their rivals but will also combine to defeat the wiles of the royal minders. No wolf pack is more ruthless or single-minded.

In former, more respectful, days such writers used to be known as court correspondents and their main task was to be on hand to accept the *Court Circular* chronicling the day-by-day engagements of the

Royal Family. They would make the front page with State visits and royal marriages, births and deaths, and then go back to reporting the royal opening of a factory or the planting of a commemorative tree which might make a few discreet lines on an inside page.

The *Court Circular* is still printed in the heavies but little else remains the same. The change started when the uncrowned Edward VIII became involved with twice married American Mrs Wallis Simpson. London was alive with rumours about their affair. British journalists knew what was going on but no newspaper printed the story because of a conspiracy of silence organized by Lord Beaverbrook after a plea from the King to spare Mrs Simpson from notoriety. Fleet Street seethed with frustration for weeks as journalists read of the King's romance in US and European publications but were forced to remain silent.

Some US magazines carrying stories about the possibility of Mrs Wallis becoming Queen of Great Britain and the Empire were censored.

What was so wrong about this conspiracy of silence was that it imposed censorship on a situation which vitally affected the future of the monarchy and the constitution of the nation.

Inevitably the story leaked and the country buzzed with rumour, but it only broke into print when the *Yorkshire Post* reported an address by the Bishop of Bradford in which he was guardedly critical of the King: 'Some of us wish that he gave more positive signs of awareness.' The *Post* then referred to foreign press reports about the romance and said: 'they plainly have a foundation in fact . . . .' And the floodgates were opened.

Writing about royalty has become big business with the specialists paying large amounts of money to anyone, especially disgruntled royal servants, with a tale to tell. Paparazzi armed with long lens cameras catch the royals in unguarded moments, and the gossip of the aristos is purveyed to the diarists. The Royal Family may be forgiven for thinking, as it does, that it is under siege by the tabloids and its advisers have recently taken action against former servants who proposed to break their contracts and 'tell all'.

It takes a certain type of mind and large resources to succeed in the tabloid end of the royal market. Sometimes, however, a freelance gets lucky. In the summer of 1991 when the Prince and Princess of Wales were cruising the Mediterranean on the yacht Alexander, which was promptly christened 'the love-boat' by the tabloids, the desperate ratpack was left behind at all the ports despite joining forces and hiring fast motor boats.

Their chagrin was complete when they were scooped by a young Italian freelance photographer, Messimo Sestini, who, with his very ordinary equipment, got the picture they were all seeking: Princess Di looking stunning in a bikini. It was estimated that Sestini would eventually make £150,000 from his pictures.

The following year, 1992, was the Queen's *annus horribilis* with the separation of the Duke and Duchess of York, the divorce of Princess Anne and Captain Mark Phillips and the announcement that the marriage of the Prince and Princess of Wales was over. There were the 'Squidgy tapes', the allegations about Charles and Camilla Parker-Bowles, the photographs of Fergie topless with her American financial adviser, and the fire at Windsor Palace.

It was truly a horrible year for the royals but a splendid one for the ratpack. Hardly a day seemed to pass without some new royal headline-making disaster. The scramble for royal stories and pictures became a feeding frenzy. The royals themselves were caught up in the madness. The Princess of Wales's most intimate friends fed information to the freelance royal reporter Andrew Morton for his best-selling *Diana: Her True Story*. Buckingham Palace tried to counteract its damaging revelations with stories about 'caring' Charles. The Queen, trying to hold back the flood of scandal which threatened to tear down her family, grudgingly accepted that she must pay income tax. Through it all, unscathed and still loved by everyone, sailed the Queen Mother, 91 and still doing her duty.

The success of Messimo Sestini and Andrew Morton, the sight of the well-paid and well-padded figure of James Whittaker, the Mirror's royal watcher – known to Princess Di as 'the big red tomato' – and the inflated sums of money offered by the tabloids for royal scandal must have been a powerful incentive to would-be freelance members of the royal ratpack. But while the rewards can be high they can also be uncertain. With so many experts in the field and so much money being thrown around not many royal scoops fall to inexperienced freelances.

Making a living out of the royals can also be a dispiriting, demeaning business involving the betrayal of confidences, hanging round the pubs favoured by royal servants and guardsmen and generally snuffling through the royal garbage.

There are, however, other ways of writing about the Royal Family which do not involve a descent into sleaze. I am not advocating a court correspondent type of kowtowing and I am certainly not suggesting a return to Mrs Simpson type censorship, but it is possible to write realistic, honest and saleable magazine features about various aspects and members of the Royal Family without compromising yourself, or putting yourself, literally, 'out of court'.

Prince Charles, emerging from the shadow of the 'retired' Diana's glamour, is, after all, the next Monarch and needs the press as much as it needs him.

His successful tour of Australasia in 1994 during which he demonstrated an admirable coolness when he was charged by one man firing blanks from a starting pistol and another spraying an air freshener, greatly improved his image and demonstrated that there is still a market for straightforward royal stories.

The interests, the foibles and the good works – especially the Princess Royal's work in the underdeveloped countries – of the Royal

Family provide constant material for a stream of royal-based magazine articles. They may not be sensational and will not make tabloid headlines but they will bring the freelance a regular supply of bread and butter with the occasional spoonful of honey.

If you decide to concentrate on royal stories then you must approach them as you would any other form of specialist writing. You must lay the groundwork, learn the history of your subject, make the contacts, get the telephone numbers, keep the files, attend all the royal events you can and record what happened even though it is not of immediate use. An afternoon watching polo on Smith's Lawn at Windsor would have provided an instant background story for the day Prince Charles fell off his polo pony and broke his arm.

Above all, get yourself recognized as a reliable royal watcher, trusted by, but not subservient to, the Buckingham Palace officials and, even more importantly, get yourself trusted by news editors.

It is worth recalling here a famous Fleet Street story of the Queen Mother's appreciation of the importance of the press. As she arrived at a civic reception to be greeted by the Lord Mayor, a typically officious local bureaucrat attempted to remove a properly accredited photographer from the red carpet where he was taking pictures. She turned away from the Mayor and called out to the official: 'Please don't do that. Mr Devon is an old friend of mine, and we both have a job to do.'

When you get to that stage in your relations with the Royal Family then you should be able to enjoy a juicy slice of the royal pie.

Of course, you may decide you would rather join the ratpack and go for the royal jugular. In which case you will need those qualities self-mockingly described by Nicholas Tomalin – killed while covering the 1973 Arab–Israeli war – as being necessary for real success in journalism: 'Ratlike cunning, a plausible manner and a little literary ability (and) the capacity to steal other people's ideas and phrases . . .'.

THE MAGAZINE ALL-ROUNDER

If writing about the royals doesn't appeal to you, choose some other speciality. Well-written, provocative articles about health, especially weight-losing diets, are always popular with magazines. So are interviews with sportsmen and women. Conservation is currently a hot subject. Fashion is a perennial.

It may be that you prefer not to specialize. In this case it is best to come to an arrangement with one magazine so that you can be the all-rounder in its team. Such an arrangement should not preclude you from writing for other magazines unless they are in direct competition. If, however, the editor wants some measure of exclusivity on your work, then he or she should pay more for it because it is, in effect, curtailing your freelance activities and cutting your income. One way of making an equitable arrangement is for the editor to guarantee you a certain number of assignments if you are a reporter or a fixed number of days' work if you are a sub-editor. You will then know precisely what you are going to earn from that source and the payments can be made on a regular monthly basis instead of story by story or day by day. It becomes, in fact, your bread and butter job.

Editors are usually content to make this sort of arrangement. They feel secure when they know they have at least one writer they can call on who is committed to them and has the mental agility to cover a variety of subjects and, in an emergency, can substitute for a specialist. It is the mark of a good journalist that he or she can seem to become an instant expert with a swift read of the cuttings.

Writing about a number of subjects can also be more enjoyable. There remains a touch of adventure about not knowing where you are going to be sent next or what type of story you are going to cover. I still get a thrill when the telephone rings and I am asked to undertake a sudden assignment outside my normal field of work.

In the space of a few months I covered events as far apart as the field gun competition at the Royal Tournament and the enthrone-ment of the Archbishop of Canterbury for the *Telegraph Magazine*. Both assignments were well-paid, interesting and in the case of the field gun competition, exciting.

I suppose the excitement of the job is the reason most of us become journalists and the desire for freedom why we become freelances. Magazine work can give both excitement and freedom as long as you can win enough assignments to survive.

11 FROM OUR LOCAL CORRESPONDENT

A local correspondent is essentially the eyes and ears of a newspaper in the area. He (or she) must be so much a part of that area that nothing moves without them knowing about it. They are to the home news desk what the stringer is to the foreign desk: a source of information, a sounding board, and a fixer when a big story breaks in the district. They are the persons who can phone the Chief Constable at home at three o'clock in the morning. They know where the local Council's skeletons are buried; about the infighting on the board of the football team. The local correspondent is often a Rotarian, a member of the golf club, an after-dinner speaker, someone who is trusted by the constituency agents of the political parties. If it is a country district the correspondent will have set up a network of village contacts – publicans and vicars make good stringers – to be kept informed.

AGENCIES

He (or she) may serve just one newspaper or put out a service duplicated to the major regional papers and to the nationals. The work can include coverage for radio and for television. Sometimes the operation becomes so big that the local correspondent will form a local news agency, a sort of mini Press Association, employing other journalists to gather and process copy.

THE LINEAGE SYSTEM

Less ambitious ones are content to work on the local newspaper and use the old-fashioned 'lineage' system, feeding the nationals with items covered in the local press, in case they are of use, and providing the regular grist of sports results and traffic conditions to various newspapers and to the agencies. When a big story breaks in their area it disturbs their quiet life but provides them with a welcome windfall as the nationals clamour for the news.

Newspapers rely heavily on their district correspondents, especially following the rationalization of Fleet Street which led to staff reductions in head offices. Most major newspapers no longer have enough reporters to send them chasing all over the country after stories. Moreover, with offices moved out of central London, the time spent in getting to a story has increased in many cases.

USING FREELANCES

So, except for the most important stories, news editors now prefer to pay trusted local freelances who can feed their copy directly into the head office's electronic system thus saving time, and economizing on reporters and expenses.

Sometimes, in an important district, a staff reporter who wants to live in the area is appointed, or the franchise is given to a retired journalist who needs the work to keep his mind and bank balance alive. It is also a traditional way for young journalists to break into the big time.

Young local correspondents who maintain a flow of good copy can expect to be invited to London for a trial or to fill in during holidays.

The ambitious ones will not only milk the local newspapers for copy but will initiate their own stories. In many cases news desks do not want the story written and are happy to pay well for a tip-off which they give to one of their own reporters to follow up.

If the local correspondent is running a general service to a number of papers he (or she) will normally send short versions of the stories to the news desks or sports desks involved. They may be used as 'nibs' or, if they are thought to be worth a bigger show, the correspondent will be asked to expand them.

The correspondent should study the market and operate on these lines. If a story will obviously be used by one newspaper and just as obviously not used by another, give it an 'exclusive' tag and sell it to the prime client. Take care, however, not to upset your other clients. Editors are funny creatures. They occasionally become enamoured of stories which are completely out of keeping with the normal character of their papers.

The local correspondent's work is essentially two-way. While you are sending in stories to news desks, news editors will be sending back queries to you. There are stories to be followed up; local angles to a story breaking elsewhere to be pursued; a picture found and transmitted; an aggrieved reader mollified; and more personal requests, 'the editor is spending the weekend in your town and would like a room overlooking the sea'. Such queries are all part of the district correspondent's day.

You will also be expected to take part in promotion campaigns, hiring venues, helping to run competitions, smoothing the path when the newspaper's advertising circus rolls into town.

THE BIG STORY

You really prove your worth, however, when a big story breaks: an air crash on a filthy night in an inaccessible part of the countryside.

Alerted by your contacts in the local emergency services and your network of village informants, you will file the first reports, giving your clients whatever you have gleaned so that they will have a few paragraphs to rush into their pages and can set their newsgathering organization in motion.

You will then put someone on phone-watch – your deputy if you have one (or someone at home) – and head for the scene of the crash. Once there, unless you have a portable telephone, your first task will be to find someone who will allow you the use of a phone; you then keep up a flow of copy until the staff reporters appear on the scene.

Your task then will be to use your local knowledge and contacts on their behalf, acting as a liaison officer, communications expert, provider of food and drink and transport manager. This part of a local correspondent's work becomes even more onerous when you are working for a television company, for their units, often four or five strong, are very demanding administratively. This admin officer role will continue until interest in the story subsides and the reporters and TV crews return to the big city. The local correspondent will then take over the story again, coming back to it in the following days and weeks with any newsworthy developments.

Similarly a correspondent in a town or city where a big political story breaks can expect to have first bite at it but when the political correspondents appear you will be relegated to a support role, feeding in local information and setting up interviews. You will take over the story again when the political circus leaves town, no doubt leaving you to massage a few dented egos among the local politicians.

USING GEOGRAPHY

A local correspondent's work takes on a somewhat different aspect when the area is newsworthy because of its geographical position and when it contains an establishment which breeds news. In the days of transatlantic liners Southampton was just such a place. Every ship sailing or docking had its quota of VIPs and showbiz people who, for some reason, always wanted to give interviews on board ship.

It was easy copy and the great ships swarmed with correspondents whose district did not extend far beyond the docks.

The scene of this sort of action has now shifted to the airports and some correspondents spend much of their working lives waiting for planes to arrive with their cargo of newsworthy passengers. The stories are similar but the conditions of work have deteriorated abysmally. There are no more drinks in splendid Verandah Deck cabins, no more leisurely interviews, no more elegance or sense of transatlantic adventure.

Security measures usually cut you off from your subject who is in a hurry either to get on the plane or to get out of the airport. A tired star, jet-lagged after a night flight, does not have the same allure as her exquisitely gowned predecessor, glowing after four days of pampered living on a transatlantic liner.

Nevertheless, any point of arrival and departure has a built-in ability to provide news and the correspondents who cover the major airports are seldom short of work.

Covering such specialized places as airports does demand a certain interest in what goes on there. It would, for example, be difficult to set up shop as a local correspondent in Canterbury without having a passing interest in the church. It would also be a mistake to open an office in Aldershot if you had no interest in the military. And anybody who decides to work at Cowes really should know the difference between a yacht and a dinghy. It is in places like this that being a local correspondent also entails being a specialist, and the area where you decide to live and work and what happens there dictates what sort of stories you are going to cover. This brings me back to the absolute necessity for a local correspondent to be part of the community, whatever sort of community it is. Fortuitously, some local correspondents even have the right name for their area. They include the excellent Braine of Oxford and Leak of Westminster.

It will be realized from this short account of the local correspondent's work that it is ideally suited for the young freelance who is trying to break into the big time, for the retired veteran, and for the journalist who is content to spend a working life outside the mainstream. It may not have the excitement of working in Fleet Street but it will probably offer a less stressful life.

GETTING STARTED

The difficulty, as with every aspect of freelancing, is getting started. All the major newspapers have a well established network of correspondents and are reluctant to alter their arrangements. You could set up shop and try to take over an area by providing a much better service than the incumbent. If so, you will find you have a fight on your hands and will have to overcome the built-in distaste that news editors have for getting rid of a trusted correspondent. You may, of course, be lucky and find an area where the resident correspondent has fallen out of favour and your entry is welcomed.

You may also find an area that it uncovered but if it is uncovered it usually means that it is not worthwhile covering and, unless you can breathe life into it where others have failed, you will have to work very hard to survive.

The normal way to become a local correspondent is through the ranks of the local paper where you will be allowed to take your cut of the lineage and become known and appreciated by the news desks of the major newspapers until you turn freelance and step into the shoes of a correspondent who has retired or finally succumbed after attending too many dinners of the local Licensees Association. Another way is to apprentice yourself to the local correspondent and become accepted as a natural successor. You could even, after a while, buy out your mentor, complete with goodwill and contacts book. The last course can work well because you will be taking over an established business trusted by its clients who will automatically telephone you when they need help in your area.

It could be expensive and would probably involve you keeping the former incumbent in comfortable retirement while you pay off the sale price from your earnings or a loan from the bank backed by a guarantee from your clients to provide you with enough work to keep the business and the loan repayments going.

GETTING PAID

Which brings us to the question of finances (see also Chapter 16). Assuming that you are a good enough journalist, sufficiently diligent and there is enough work available there is no reason why you should not earn a comfortable living as a freelance local correspondent.

The normal method of payment for a well-established correspondent is by an arranged retainer plus a payment for every story or tip-off accepted. Time spent assisting reporters from the head office or carrying out special assignments will either be paid for on a daily basis or with a lump sum.

The rates will vary according to the strength and the exclusivity of the story and the current financial state of the newspaper involved. It is normally the job on any newspaper of a senior member of a newsdesk and a member of the accounts staff dealing with contributions to go though the pages of each edition and the copy submitted every day and mark it up with the prices to be paid for the freelance copy, based on the agreed rates, which can be by the line i.e. lineage.

There is an element of chance in this system. You may have had a row with the man doing the marking-up or he may have had a quarrel with his wife is which case you might suffer financially. Some payments might also slip between the floorboards with stories not being recognized as freelance work, or ordered stories not being used and not appearing on the tally sheet.

KEEPING ACCOUNTS

You must, therefore, as a local correspondent, keep an impeccable account of the work you do. Every story, every tip-off, every request for information and every bit of assistance must be logged along with the name of the person and newspaper involved. Each item must be timed and dated and if you have come to an agreement over a special fee that, too, must be noted.

Then, when your monthly account comes in you must check it against your own books. This is especially important for a local correspondent for, unlike a magazine freelance whose payments tend to be large and few, the local correspondent's income is more likely to be made up of many small payments and it is only too easy for them to get lost at source in the haste of producing a newspaper, especially if a story is switched from one department to another. A story which starts out as news and ends the night as a feature is a certain candidate for accountancy confusion.

You must also keep a careful account, complete with invoices and receipts, of all the expenses you have incurred in covering ordered stories and complying with requests for assistance. Get them done and submitted as soon as possible. Items get forgotten as the days pass by and news editors, whose gratitude for your help may be expansive on the day of the story, become more querulous about expenses as the memory of the story fades.

The price of survival as a freelance, especially as a local correspondent, is eternal vigilance over the accounts. The thing to remember, as I have emphasized throughout this book, is that you are running a business just like any other business. This does not mean to say that you should not have fun within your chosen metier.

As a journalist with the ear of editors in London you could, if you so desired, exercise considerable political and social power in your community. You will be a welcome guest at most functions both because of the power of publicity and because members of the public love to hear stories about newspapers and newspapermen – the more wicked the better. It may be a small pool but you will be a big fish in it and when the big story breaks locally you will have plenty of excitement to keep the adrenalin flowing.

12 GOSSIP COLUMNS

Gossip columns are often sneered at even by journalists. They are referred to as being boring, the dustbin for stories that could not get into any other part of the paper on merit; of being a pay-off for press agents' hospitality; of purveying sleazy tittle-tattle; or a combination of all these faults.

How agreeable it must be to be able to afford such high-minded distaste. It should never be forgotten, however, that a good gossip column can sell newspapers. People leading very ordinary lives look to the columnists to give them glimpses of a life they will never see for themselves. It does not matter that the lives they lead are probably far more rewarding than those of the bimbos and poseurs that appear in the column. The glitter, the excitement, the sense of danger that emerges from the columns keep them fascinated. They feel that, even at second hand, they are part of Nigel Dempster's world.

Lord Beaverbrook had no doubts about the importance of gossip columns. He used the columns in his newspapers, especially the *Evening Standard* diary, as vehicles for his private vendettas and the planting of political stories. He would put stories in the diary which would have made page one splashes in other newspapers. Under his rule the *Evening Standard* diary, William Hickey in the *Daily Express* and Crossbencher in the *Sunday Express* became required reading for any aspiring politician or member of London Society.

He staffed them with young men and women who had caught his eye. Many of them went on to become Fleet Street luminaries. None of the present-day proprietors have the same interest in their gossip columns but the columns remain a vital part of a newspaper's daily mix.

They also remain an important training ground for young journalists. The need to work accurately under pressure, to write concisely but with style and to build a circle of influential contacts is inherent in working for a diary.

They are also happy hunting grounds for freelance journalists who have cracked the code of writing diary paragraphs. Short, and usually picked up on the periphery of another story, a diary item costs little in time and effort and is almost all profit. A freelance friend of mine, a respected political writer, would never leave his house in the morning before earning his lunch money by selling an item to a column. He would do this by reading the political news of the day and then composing a paragraph about one of the people involved, using his own knowledge of that person and a couple of judicious telephone calls to top up the story.

Let me give you an example from my own experience. Following the death of Llewellyn Thompson, a former US Ambassador to

Moscow, the obituary columns carried full accounts of his life and times as a diplomat but none of them mentioned his love of playing poker so I was able to write a diary story about the poker games he used to hold every Sunday evening in the Moscow embassy. It was a simple enough story, taken straight out of my own memory of those games, but it was eagerly accepted by the *Daily Telegraph's* Peterborough column and made a readable paragraph.

It is remarkable how much material these columns eat up and columnists, however brilliant, will occasionally have days when they look in despair at the blank screen and know that they have nothing to write. It was on one such hot, summer's Sunday morning when I was writing the late, lamented William Hickey column in the *Daily Express* and could not uncover a single useable paragraph in the file. At that moment a number 15 bus went past the office window and in a moment of blind despair I rushed out, caught the next number 15 to arrive, rode it to the end of the line and wrote a whole column about my journey – it was in the days before Hickey became preoccupied with the tinsel lives of tinsel people. It turned out rather well but I would not have done it if a freelance contributor had telephoned with a useable story.

On another, shaming, occasion I crumpled up a story contributed by one of my colleagues and threw it into the waste-paper basket snarling that it was unprintable rubbish. By the end of the day there was such a dearth of copy that I had to delve in the bin, retrieve it and smooth out the wrinkles so that it could become the lead to the column. My colleague had the good grace to accept my apologies.

In fact some of the columns in the nation dailies now have staffs of four or five journalists, devoted to providing material for one small section of the paper, but it is a specialized section and it has to be produced six times a week; there is always room, therefore, for good material to force its way in and occasionally, as we have seen, for some not so good material being rescued to save the column.

Sundays and holidays, especially the ever-lengthening Christmas, are the worst times for diary writers so it will pay to save up a stock of timeless items for those days. These are stories which might not get in during a busy week but which will earn you a diary editor's undying gratitude when the whole world seems to have gone to sleep. The lesson is: never throw away a timeless story; it will find a niche one day.

Diary paragraphs do not have to be about the so-called glitterati. Columns like Peterborough, *The Times* diary and the *Evening Standard* diary range wide and their interests are reflected, if with a smaller scope, in provincial newspapers. Politics, sport, the arts, anything of interest to a varied readership can find a place in these columns. All that one needs to write a paragraph is a recognizable name, some interesting circumstances and a peg of news on which to hang them. The late Hugo Wortham, who wrote the Peterborough column for many years and trained a whole generation of diarists, used to say that the ideal paragraph contained one name, one fact and one error. The error was to encourage readers to write corrective letters, thus providing yet more paragraphs.

It is remarkable what extraordinary stories will emerge if you write a paragraph about some long-forgotten military campaign or a sporting occasion in a far-away place. It is one of the laws of column writing that however obscure the subject there is always at least one reader happy to provide a definitive account of the incident – and several others even happier to prove him wrong.

Such historical items obviously need to have up-to-date pegs on which they can be hung but according to Wortham's law, once you have the peg the rest follows as night follows day.

THE DIARY STORY

For many staff writers their newspaper's column is a nuisance. On slack days specialists are badgered by editors to provide material for it and it can also become a ragbag into which unwanted material is placed. This drives the diary editor to despair, leads the editor to threaten to close it down and provides a rich field for freelances. It is, however, a field which often goes untilled because the freelance mind is often not conditioned to diary work. Whenever you go out on a story, whenever you interview somebody, whenever you review a book, you should always keep in your mind the thought that apart from the main story, the material for a diary story for a grateful newspaper will almost certainly emerge.

Let us suppose the Queen is visiting your city to open a new factory and you notice that her personal detective is wearing the same old school tie as the managing director of the factory and it emerges that they were schoolmates. It is a curiosity which has no place in your main story, but, dressed up with quotes from both men, will make an excellent diary story.

After dinner speeches are an excellent source of diary material. You only need one witty remark by a speaker with a recognizable name to make a usable paragraph. The former Bishop of Barking,

Jim Roxburgh, provided *The Times* diary with a fine example when he told a dinner gathering of the occasion when he was presiding at a school prize giving and a young woman tripped while mounting the platform.

With true Christian charity he helped her to her feet remarking: 'This is the first time I have ever had a fallen woman in my arms.' To which she replied: 'And I've never been picked up by a bishop before.'

A combination of a titled or showbiz speaker, a notable venue, a charitable cause and a smart speech writer is manna from heaven for a freelance diarist. Memorial services are an equally good source of diary material. It is remarkable what splendid stories, too often ignored, are told in eulogies.

The big hotels are an ever-flowing well of diary material. They have public relations officers who are always anxious to get their establishment's name and clients suitably mentioned, and they are filled with a constantly changing clientele, many of whom are equally anxious to get their names mentioned. Getting to know your way around the hotels also helps when a story breaks which they are not so anxious to have publicized. Cultivating the hotels is as profitable in the provinces as it is in London.

Book reviewing is another way of gathering diary material. Very few books out of the thousands that are published actually get into the review pages but they often contain excellent diary stories, especially if they are biographies. If you manage to get yourself on a publisher's list, they will be quite happy to keep sending you books in exchange for columnar publicity.

It is a good way, not only of acquiring stories, but of stocking your bookshelves. Some booksellers also buy review copies at a discount thus providing an excellent source of emergency income.

You should not ignore the fact that there is more than one type of diary. There are business diaries, arts diaries, sports diaries, as many diaries as there are types of publications or sections in a newspaper, and they add up to a great number of column inches which all have to be filled.

STYLE AND CODE

Each column has its own style and preferences for stories. There is no point in firing stories off in the general direction of the column. Your arrows have to be meticulously aimed. To make sure of scoring, you must analyse your target columns, break their code and then give them stories which slot neatly into their format. Some stories will suit a number of columns. Always ask the diary editor if he or she wants the story before writing it so that, if accepted, it becomes 'ordered' and the paper is committed to paying for it. You can then write the paragraph in the appropriate style for that column. If that diary editor does not want it you can then try a rival paper. Some diary editors with a distinctive style are happy to pay for the bare bones of a story, preferring to write the paragraphs themselves rather than rewrite your attempts to match the column's style.

It should not be forgotten that provincial newspapers and the specialist publications have diaries as well as the nationals, although the payments are not as great. It is surprising, however, how the payments mount if you can maintain a flow of printable items. It is not a bad idea to keep your payments for diary items in a separate account to be used for a holiday or an unexpected expense.

One of the best-selling items for freelance diarists is the amusing tailpiece which rounds off the column, especially if it lends itself to a witty headline. Few diary editors could resist this example which was lifted from a church notice board in Bolton and appeared in the *Daily Telegraph*: 'Sunday rota. Coffee and biscuits: K. O'Shaughnessy. Monday talk: "Lord have mercy . . .".' It carried the headline: 'Last Cuppa'.

This may seem small beer but a tailpiece is an integral part of most columns and it is frustratingly difficult to find one for every day. Columnists often spend as much time in the search for a suitable last paragraph as they do in acquiring a lead story and if you are tuned in to their needs, these little items can provide an easy source of income.

THE SPECIAL COLUMNIST

Some freelances may aspire to writing their own gossip column. It is an ambition to be approached with caution. I once wrote a column called 'Chandelier London' about Mayfair nightlife for the *Daily Express*. I spent the day organizing the night's activities then put on a dinner jacket and started the night's round of cocktail parties, dinners and dances before writing the column for the midnight edition. It was a killer; by the end of the 'season' I was exhausted. I never wanted to see a canapé, or listen to an after-dinner speech again. Such a column needs a staff of three or four and I would suggest that it would be impossible for one writer to sustain, especially if you do not have the resources of a major publication plus the power of its name. It is one thing to request tickets to a dinner in the name of the *Daily Bugle*, and quite another to ask for them in the name of Jim Bloggs.

There are some successful freelance gossip columnists but they are mainly in the USA where their columns, along with columns dealing with politics, foreign affairs, sport, and the arts, are syndicated to newspapers around the country. There is no truly national press in the USA. The country is so large and diverse that each town relies on its own paper which fills its pages with local news, agency copy and the syndicated columns.

Each newspaper pays a modest amount for the column but, if it is successful, literally hundreds of newspapers buy the column which is syndicated through an agency, and all those modest amounts add up to a great deal of money. The columnist is then able to afford a staff of researchers and reporters and, as with the Hollywood columnists, exercises a great deal of power.

This system does not work in Britain because the country is too small and the system of having national and provincial newspapers means that the staff columnists on the nationals can be read in every part of the country. The British editors' love of exclusivity means they simply will not buy a column which can be read in another newspaper bought on the same news-stand as their own.

There are successful freelance columnists in Britain but they are mainly writers who have achieved fame as staff writers and have become so valuable they have been able to make a freelance deal with their proprietors or sell themselves and their column to a rival newspaper in a freelance package. If you intend to follow that path, I commend your ambition but it is a long, hard road and not many reach the summit. But, do not forget, even the most glittering of columnists need tailpieces.

13 FREELANCING AND THE SPOKEN WORD

One of the joys of being a freelance is that there are many different ways of making a living, often using the same material. The staff reporter usually does not bother to pursue these alternative avenues because, as long as he or she does the work to the editor's satisfaction, the pay cheque arrives every month, but the freelance must be alive to every opportunity and if these can be combined with self-projection, then so much the better.

SPEECH-MAKING

The particular opportunities I have in mind are speech-making, radio and television. Many journalists get asked to make after-dinner speeches to the local Rotarians or young wives club and get a free meal and, if they are lucky, a bottle of whisky for their trouble. That's fine if you are charitably minded, but if you have got something to say that people find interesting then speech-making should become as much part of your freelance business as writing. You are using all the same material and information as in your writing except that you must now add the talent of speaking. So why should you not be paid for it?

I am not suggesting you should charge your local charitable organizations for saying a few words but there are large lunching and dining clubs who think nothing of paying £250 for being amused and interested for half an hour over their coffee.

I know a doctor who makes a sizeable secondary income by talking about medical disasters at golf club dinners. Some sporting personalities command fees of up to £1000 for a speech. Some of the richer women's clubs will pay travelling expenses and put you up as well as paying your fee.

As you might expect, none of this is done on a haphazard basis. There are agencies which supply speakers for functions and they need to be assured that you can perform satisfactorily before they will engage you. It is show business, after all, and before they let you loose on their circuit they will need to vet your material and make sure that you can actually get up on your hind legs and communicate. If you can't communicate, if your mouth dries up and your mind goes blank and you have an attack of the vapours when you see all those expectant faces in front of you, then forget it. Public speaking is not for you.

If, on the other hand, you find your audience laughing with you instead of at you and you can sense them settling down to enjoy themselves, you can look forward to a profitable and enjoyable sideline to your career as a freelance. Good speakers are in great demand and the news soon gets around the dining circuit if you can entertain a well-fed and well-watered audience determined to get value for their money.

Once that starts to happen, your agent should be able to book you for one or two functions every week during the speaking season. If you are really good at it and have a topical subject and a good deal of knowledge and experience on it you might land a lecture tour of the USA which is exhausting but highly profitable.

The beauty of moving round the circuit is that you rarely speak to the same people more than once a year so that you can use the same talk for a whole year, which really is making the optimum use of your material. You may, in fact, need two speeches, one for women's luncheon clubs and the other for the annual dinner of the local police force and similar high-spirited occasions.

It pays to be flexible. I was once asked to address a charity organization and had prepared my usual light-hearted account of a foreign correspondent's life which always seemed to be appreciated on such occasions. I realized that I was probably working to the wrong script as soon as I arrived and was shown into a huge marquee on a rolling lawn and had a glass of excellent champagne put into my hand. There seemed, I thought, to be rather a lot of distinguished men and grand women present for a simple charity do and halfway through a splendid dinner it became apparent that my audience was composed of diplomats, senior officers in the services, men who were very definitely something in the city and their equally accomplished wives and my pleasant little suburban speech would not do at all.

I had to excuse myself, disappear into the elegant Portakabin loo and spend the next five minutes scrambling together a powerful piece about terrorism and the state of the world. I got back just in time to prevent my hostess panicking because she thought I had taken fright and run away. In the end, it all went very well, but I learnt two lessons that night: never under-estimate your audience and always be prepared for the unexpected.

That was exceptional. On most occasions people are content to be entertained by tales about journalism. Even those who profess to loath 'the meedja' are fascinated by the story behind the story, the sort of tales that journalists tell each other in the pub but which rarely find their way into print. Audiences tend to live vicariously, savouring the thrills, dangers and glitter of the job. For that reason crime reporters make popular speakers, so do women war correspondents and gossip columnists.

I find that a good recipe is never to speak for more than thirty minutes and always leave plenty of time for questions. The audience is a funny beast, it is slow to get warmed up but once it starts asking questions it is very difficult to stop.

Try not to read your speech; nothing is more off-putting than a speaker reading every syllable from a prepared script. It is much better to have a series of memo cards which you can glace at while you are actually communicating with your audience. The best talks, like the best stories, should be delivered as if you were speaking to someone you know well. Audiences, like readers, have to feel involved. They like to be looked at. Make them laugh, if you can, very early on. They will grant you a lot of leeway in exchange for laughter but never insult their intelligence with a series of weak jokes.

Speak up, aim your voice at the back of the hall and if it is sufficiently powerful, put the microphone aside. It shows you are confident and audiences like that, but make sure they can hear you. Speak clearly, do not gabble, breathe properly and use short sentences. Above all, remember that they have paid good money to be entertained. So entertain them.

RADIO WORK

The amount of radio work available to journalists has increased many-fold since the advent of local radio and these stations are ideal places for young freelances to learn the skills of broadcasting while covering local news and interviewing for the station's own current affairs programmes. A local radio station is very similar to a local newspaper and demands the same local knowledge and coverage aimed at a small area.

Journalists working in the news room of a radio station or sub-editing copy will be doing almost exactly the same job as if they were working on a newspaper. Where they differ, of course, is that a radio reporter needs to possess the skills of public speaking as well as reporting. No matter how good a reporter you are, you will be no good on radio if people cannot understand what you are saying. A clear speaking voice, and the ability to express your thoughts in an orderly fashion are essential.

You also need to be able to think fast on your feet for when you are broadcasting live, you cannot press the delete button and rewrite your story if you make a mistake. It has already gone, flashing through the ether, to be picked up by listeners a milli-second later. You must also be concise, for you often have only a couple of minutes to tell your story. You also need a special skill in interviewing. A newspaper reporter can spend time over an interview and mould the quotes to a story but when a radio or television reporter is interviewing live he needs a 'sound-bite', a short quote which either encapsulates the essence of the story or causes a sensation. Some politicians and professional publicists understand the value of 'sound-bites' and go to interviews with a pocketful already prepared, and the interviewer is duly grateful.

It is more difficult when interviewing members of the public. They usually have to be led into using the 'sound-bite' the interviewer wants and that requires much skill. If the interviewer has time it becomes much simpler but when only one short quote is used out of a longish interview it can lead to angry accusations of selective reporting.

That said, freelancing in radio journalism follows much the same pattern as freelancing for newspapers and magazines. The main problem remains getting started in the profession. The BBC runs much sought after training courses in both television and radio, but these are not available to freelances. One way in is by taking a job as a studio 'gofer' in which you 'go for' the tea and do all the menial tasks such as setting up the studio for interviews and making sure the waterjugs are filled to drown the all too frequent frogs in the throat. In this way you learn the business as you would as a junior reporter on a local paper. The young people who do this usually build up a presentation tape on which they record their best radio work in order to impress potential employers. It is the radio equivalent of the reporter's cuttings book.

Another way is by establishing yourself as a print journalist before moving across to radio to do exactly the same job in a different medium. The studio machinery and the need to carry recording equipment may seem daunting at first but the modern journalist's experience of tape recorders, word processors and visual display units linked to their newspapers' electronic copy system makes the transition reasonably painless.

The other way to make the transition into radio is to become an expert on a certain subject, capable of producing an instant opinion at the break of a story.

Sometimes this happens at great speed. It is rather disconcerting to be lying in bed listening to the 'Today' programme at seven in the morning when the telephone rings and it is one of the programme editors asking if you would appear on the programme. 'When?' you ask. 'Now', they say and you are on the air, speaking into the telephone on one side of the bed while your words are coming out of the radio on the other side. One of the problems of this type of crash interview is that it usually happens in the early morning before you have put your voice on and before you have properly grasped the significance of the event about which you are being questioned. I find the best way to deal with this situation is to be absolutely assertive and confident and, if I am asked a difficult question, I use the politician's trick of answering a completely different question, which I have not been asked.

The advantage of these early morning interviews is that all news editors listen to them and they will arrive in their offices with the name of an expert capable of dealing with one of the day's breaking stories already implanted in their consciousness. It soothes their anxiety ulcers to know they have a certain supply of words only a telephone number away. So you are likely to get a profitable assignment as the result of two or three minutes' talking over the telephone while you are finishing your early morning tea in bed.

This knock-on effect spreads throughout the radio world. If you appear on one programme you are quite likely to be asked to appear on others while your subject is news. If you appear on 'Today', then it is quite likely that Radio Scotland, the 'World at One' and the World Service will ask you to contribute your expertise to their programmes. It does not matter that you will be saying much the same thing. They have to cover the story, their audiences are different and they have someone who has shown some knowledge of the subject and an ability to broadcast. This is sufficient. You will then go down on the lists kept by programme assistants as the person to be called when your subject becomes news again.

This can lead to being asked to join in a studio discussion or be interviewed at length at a later date. This enables you to prepare properly and to do some lateral thinking instead of simply answering a series of crash questions. It also gives you the opportunity to be provocative, although, since most of these programmes are recorded, if you are too provocative you will be erased.

It is all very seductive and it gives your ego a great fillip when people come up to you in the street and say, 'I heard you on the radio. You were very good.' Of course, if you are silly enough to ask their opinion of what you said they will get embarrassed and say: 'Well, I didn't actually listen to what you said, but you sounded very good.'

It is now that you must remember that you are a freelance and that you are not broadcasting to 'sound very good' but as part of your efforts to prosper as a journalist. Too often, producers of programmes will try to use your expertise without paying for it. Do not allow them to get away with it. Make it plain that the moment they ring you, even if it is only to consult you about a programme, the taximeter is running. They would not dream of working without being paid so why should you?

Some programme executives are impeccable in making arrangements for payment, others tend to think you should be honoured to be asked to share their air-time. Do not give in to this arrogance. If you are considered worthy of being asked to appear, you are worthy of being paid.

You must also make sure you claim the travelling expenses due to you. The normal BBC procedure is to send you a contract after you have made your contribution setting out the payment due to you calculated on the amount of time you were on the air. Expenses and 'disturbance payments' are also included in the contract. If there are special reasons why you should be paid more – you may have acted as a consultant to the programme as well as appearing – then you have to make a separate deal. One of the anomalies of working for the BBC is that different sections of the organization pay different rates for precisely the same story. I have on occasion done the same story on the same day for programmes in Scotland and in London and the Scots have always paid better.

Provision is made in the contract for VAT to be paid under the self-billing system (I write about VAT at greater length in Chaper 16). You then sign one copy of the contract and return it to the BBC and you will receive your cheque. If you need the money in a hurry – and most freelances are sometimes in that situation – you can take signed copy to a BBC accounts department and get paid over the counter.

If you make the breakthrough as a freelance radio journalist, the next step is to write and present your own programmes. These will not necessarily be of a journalistic nature but they will probably be based on the contacts you have made and the expertise you have acquired in your journalistic work. If you reach this happy stage in your freelance career then it is time to bring in your agent and accountant to make sure you are getting a fair slice of the cake, that you don't eat it all at once and that there are bigger and better cakes to come.

Most of the successful freelances in radio work according to terms governed by a contract. A fresh contract is drawn up when you embark on a new project. This means that you can negotiate new and better terms. It also means that you can be dropped if you or your work are no longer needed. This is a situation which neatly sums up the advantages and perils of being a freelance.

TV WORK

Freelancing for television follows much the same pattern as radio work, the great difference being that while you can work for radio by telephone, you need a camera and its crew in order to appear on television. If you have the necessary training and experience and have been hired on a freelance basis as a reporter this will be no problem, for you will be assigned a cameraman, a soundman and whatever other crew is deemed necessary. If, however, you appear for what you know rather than your television expertise it means that either the crew must come to you or you must go to a studio.

All this may seem self-evident but it does considerably complicate a freelance's life. Much depends on where you live. If you are in taxi-distance of the studio there is no problem, but if, like me, you are more than an hour's drive from the nearest studio it means that you lose a considerable part of the day for what is rarely more than a few minutes on the screen. On a number of occasions when TV AM wanted me to appear on their early morning show to discuss Middle Eastern affairs they would send a car all the way from London to my home near the south coast, take me to London, put me up at a hotel and then drive me back after the show the next morning for an appearance of five minutes at the most.

It was certainly disruptive for me but it paid well, and, more importantly, the 'knock-on' effect of having appeared on television is even greater than that of having appeared on radio. Once television has projected you into the nation's consciousness as an expert in your field your telephone will start to ring with calls from commissioning editors anxious to buy your services. They want you not so much because you are an expert but because television has said you are an expert. Other television shows will also want you if you 'come over' well and your name will be entered in the lists of potential performers kept by programme assistants. It is all a bit incestuous. If it happens, make the most of it. Television fame is immediate. It can also be short-lived.

As in radio there are producers who think that the act of appearing, the television ego-trip, is reward enough for a journalist. I was once asked if I would be interviewed about events in the Middle East by the London office of a major US television company. I agreed but when I asked them how much they paid for such interviews they were quite shocked. 'We never pay members of the public for interviews' said the producer. 'But I am not a member of the public', I replied, 'I am a professional journalist specializing in this field and you are buying my services.' He refused to pay and so I refused to do the interview. This brings us back to the basic law of freelancing: never work without pay.

Another trick you must guard against is when a programme assistant telephones you to ask your advice about a potential programme and you find yourself acting as a consultant, giving away all your hard-won expertise without any guarantee of a consultancy view or appearance money. If this happens then make it plain that unless they agree to paying a consultant's fee they will have to do without your expertise.

You may think this dangerous advice, especially if you are desperately anxious for any opening into television, but you must keep your nerve. More openings are created by maintaining your independence and making yourself wanted than by allowing yourself to be conned by production assistants.

Certainly there is a good career to be carved out of television either behind the cameras as a writer, consultant or sub-editor, or on screen as a reporter or presenter. It should not be thought that a presenter is just a pretty face reading other people's words. The job often involves a great deal of journalism. Angela Rippon is a fine example of the successful TV freelance. Not only does she look good as a presenter, she is also an excellent reporter and uses her journalistic skills in a number of programmes.

The independent companies that make documentary films are always in need of journalists and, because of their own freelance way of working, prefer to hire people for specific projects.

Such work can be very rewarding professionally and financially. The trick is to maintain the flow of work without the wild swings from feast to famine which can make a freelance's life sometimes too exciting, even perilous.

If, of course, you reach the heights of TV eminence scaled by the Dimblebys you will have no problems with workflow, and you will probably turn down more contracts than you accept. Alas, there is not room for many people on that summit. Nevertheless, there are some comfortable crags on which you can perch as long as you are properly equipped and trained. As with every other aspect of journalism, success in television depends on a sound training, enthusiasm, self-discipline and an affinity with the medium you have chosen.

14 BRANCHING OUT INTO BOOKS

There comes a time in most freelances' lives when they get an uncontrollable urge to write a book, while other journalists become freelances in order to give themselves the time and freedom to write 'the great novel'.

My first reaction is to say: don't. Writing a book is hard graft and in most cases the equation of time and labour and anguish measured against the monetary rewards of authorship make it ridiculously unrewarding quite apart from diverting your energies from profitable freelancing.

Sometimes it pays off. *The Day of the Jackal* marked the metamorphosis of Frederick Forsyth from agency reporter to millionaire thriller writer. He did it the hard way. The 'Jackal', his first manuscript, was turned down by a number of publishers before it was eventually accepted.

Such success is sweet and profitable when it comes. It does not come very often, however, and few journalists find themselves in the position of being able to abandon their trade to become full-time authors. If they do not catch the attention of the reading public or are not lucky enough to hit the literary fashion of the day, the normal reward for much hard work is sales of a few thousand.

Fiction writers might get some decent reviews from their friends and have the satisfaction of seeing their work on the bookshelves; they can now call themselves novelists but it is not likely to impress their bank managers.

Factual writers get more tangible rewards by being recognized as experts in their subject and therefore being asked to write articles and lecture and be listed by television researchers as people to be telephoned to take part in discussion programmes when their subject becomes news. An 'expert' who has written a book becomes immediate television material. The very fact that your words have appeared between hard covers gives you instant credibility, but it is reaction to the publication of your book, not the book itself which pays off.

Most would-be authors quite rightly ignore these warnings; the urge to write is overwhelming. You have a brilliant idea, you know that you can write like an angel and you are confident you will sell hundreds of thousands of copies; but how do you set about getting it published?

AGENTS

The first thing you should do is to acquire an agent. No matter how long you have been a journalist you still need a professional to guide your steps through the publishing jungle.

Discuss your idea with your agent. You may have a basically good story to tell but be approaching it from the wrong angle. Listen to your agent; after all, that is why you are employing one and it is in your agent's interests to get you published. If you find you are incompatible you can always find another agent.

If your agent agrees that you have a viable product, he or she will require a synopsis from you and, if you are a first-time author, a sample chapter just to prove to the publisher that you can put words together in the right order.

THE BOOK SYNOPSIS

Some would-be authors baulk at the thought of doing a synopsis. This is a fundamental error for the synopsis is the selling point of your work. It shows the publisher what you plan to do and it provides the publisher with a basis on which to decide not only whether to buy your book but also what sort of contract and how big an advance to offer you.

The synopsis has to be concise but informative with a general introduction outlining the book followed by a summary of each chapter. About 50 words for each chapter should be sufficient. Presentation is important; after all, you are selling yourself as well as your book. The publisher has to be assured that you are a responsible citizen who will fulfil the terms of your contract, and deliver the agreed number of words in a publishable form by an agreed date.

The first page should carry the working title and your name neatly set out in the middle of a decent sheet of paper. The synopsis follows on with its chapters numbered and titled.

I find that writing a synopsis is invaluable, not only as a means of selling a book to a publisher but also as a way of clearing one's thoughts about it. You may have done a great deal of research, filled files with notes, even sketched out chapters, but you have not yet seen the book as a whole. In fact what started as a simple, clear idea may by now be in a state of total confusion. When you have done the synopsis, there is the whole book laid out in front of you in summary form and you can see its strengths and weaknesses. You may alter it as you go along, adding and subtracting, but the blueprint is still there to guide you.

THE CONTRACT

Once you have written the synopsis, the action passes to your agent, who may ask you to make some alterations to appeal to a particular publisher. Then it is up to the agent to sell it. If the publisher is interested a meeting is arranged, and then your agent can start haggling over the terms of the contract: the advance, the royalties, date of completion, overseas rights and serial rights, who is going to pay for the pictures and the index.

It is better that the author stays out of the negotiations not only because the agent is more experienced in these matters but also because, if things go sour, the agent will act as a buffer between you and the publisher.

Most publishers have a standard contract which has been perfected over years of haggling with agents so most of the discussion turns on percentages. Where the agent really earns his commission is in screwing as big an advance as possible out of the publisher. This advance is usually paid in three tranches: the first on signing the contract, the second on delivering the manuscript in usable form and the third on publication.

This advance is set against the royalties earned from the sales of the book. Very often the advance is all that an author will earn so it is important to get as large an advance as possible. Anything earned above the advance means that the book has 'washed its face' and may be regarded as a success. The author will also receive a percentage – agreed by his agent – from any overseas rights, serial rights and television and radio rights. Serial rights in one of the 'heavy' Sunday newspapers usually ensure the success of a book. Not only can they bring in up to £50,000 and sometimes more, they also stimulate sales in the bookshops. The publisher and the agent will, of course, take their cut of the proceeds.

COMMISSIONED WORK

It may be that a publisher will approach you to write a book after seeing something you have written. This makes the negotiations easier because the publisher will have a clear idea of what is wanted and you do not have to sell yourself and your idea.

Strangely enough, it does not make the writing any easier. I was asked to write a book of some 80,000 words on the Black September group following a series I had written on the group for the *Sunday Telegraph*. I thought it would be easy. I had already written 20,000 words in the series; all I would need to do would be to write four words for every one. But it does not work like that. Words are not like a piece of elastic which can be stretched and stretched.

Writing a book requires a completely different technique from the journalistic disciplines of writing a self-contained article or series of articles each one of which can stand alone. Where an article might skim over sections of the developing plot, carrying the reader along by sheer pace, a book has to explain why and how and should present a seamless account.

I found that the only thing to do with the Black September series was to dismantle it into its component parts, do much more research and interviewing and then reassemble the structure in a completely different way, building in the new material.

ORGANIZING YOUR TIME

The keys to writing a book, especially a factual book, are organization and discipline. You must organize your material in chapter form before you start writing otherwise you will find yourself in a terrible muddle with bits of paper covering your desk, while you search for notes which have disappeared. The discipline comes with setting yourself targets. Contracts usually give writers a year to complete a book. At first this seems more than adequate and writers, having accepted their advance, are tempted to put the book on one side while they carry out other, more immediately profitable, work.

Others simply do nothing until the advance is spent. The weeks slip by, then comes the moment of realization: you only have a few weeks in which to do a year's work. It is much better to set yourself a daily target of words at the outset and do your best to maintain that target.

It is remarkable how the words tick away to the required number – usually about 90,000. I know how difficult it is to maintain the schedule especially when the sun is shining and the fish are biting but it is very reassuring when you know that you will be able to finish the book on a certain day.

It is advisable while you are maintaining your schedule to keep a record of what you have put into each chapter. It is very easy to forget what you have written when you are engaged in a major project especially when it is on disc and not paper.

You will find yourself either telling the same story twice or missing it out so that you will come across it all forlorn after you have finished the book and have to squeeze it in where it may not fit so comfortably.

With this record of completed chapters you will be able to make a quick check against your synopsis and see exactly what you have done and what still needs to be done without scrolling back through your discs or reading through everything you have written so far.

GETTING THE WORDS FLOWING

There will be dark days when nothing seems to go right, days when you stare at the virgin sheet of paper or the empty screen and cannot produce a single word, days when you despair of ever finishing your masterpiece; but you must never give up. Tear up everything you have written and start again, but never give up.

When I am stuck I go for a long walk with my dog and usually by the time I have returned the problems which seemed so insoluble have resolved themselves. I take a small tape-recorder with me so that if I get struck by literary lightning I am able to record my thoughts before I am distracted and forget them.

Another trick of the trade I use when the words simply will not come is to write anything just to get the words flowing: a favourite poem, a quotation, a description of the scene outside the window – it does not matter what it is – and then plunge into the story. You can always come back and take out the unwanted words and tidy up your prose, especially on screen.

REMEMBERING THE BREAD

It is important, however, not to become so involved with writing your book that you neglect your journalism. It may well be that you will turn out a best-seller and you will never have to do day-to-day journalism ever again; but you do not know this and if you do not earn your daily bread you will find your advance for the book disappearing like ice on the equator with nothing replacing it.

You will also find that your contacts drop away. People quickly forget you are a freelance unless you come up with stories and ideas, and they become accustomed to running their publications without you. Your journalistic administration will also suffer. It is boring to cut the newspapers and keep your files up to date when you are excited by your book but unless you do so you will find that when the book is finished and is possibly not the best-seller you had hoped for you will have to build up your freelance business all over again.

It is better therefore to treat your book writing as just one department of your business. Write 1,000 words a day then put it on one side while you get on with your journalism.

When your books are a success you will be able to wean yourself from journalism if that is what you want, but until then remember it is your meal ticket. I realize that this advice will be scorned by those who would prefer to starve in a garret for their art's sake, but this book is written as a survival course for freelances not as an ego-massaging exercise for aesthetes.

PUSHING YOUR SALES

You finish your book and you hand it over – two copies to the publisher, one to your agent, or, if they are up to date, a set of disks to each.

You might think all your hard work is over. Not so. There is a foreword to be written, publicity material to be compiled, a bibliography to be listed, pictures to be chosen, the dust jacket to be discussed. Then the edited proofs appear and are wanted back with your corrections within days.

You have now reached the stage where your good relations with the publisher come under strain. Do not be bullied. Take your time and make sure the manuscript is as you want it.

By all means allow the editor to make corrections to your grammar and punctuation but not to make substantial changes to your text without first discussing them with you. The changes may be beneficial but that is not the point: the book is yours and you are responsible for what it contains. If need be, sit down with the editor and argue your way through the book line by line. Always remember, however, that under the terms of your contract the publishers will normally have the right to refuse to produce your book if it does not fulfil their expectations and you may be faced with the options of rewriting, accepting the editor's revisions or not getting the book published.

Remember not to make excessive author's corrections on your sheet proofs. Publishers hate major revisions; they are costly and time-consuming, so it is important to get the book right before you submit it even if it means asking for more time.

All problems resolved, the proofs vanish to the printers and suddenly one day a padded package arrives in the post, the first copy of your first book. It is a proud moment, but now it is back to work for you will have to do your best to sell it by publicizing it.

The circus starts with a publishing party – red wine and canapés in an establishment suitable to the amount of money the publishers have allocated for bringing your book to the attention of the public.

You are supposed to charm 'the trade' and persuade the invited book reviewers to write kind words about you and your book but it usually turns into a free-for-all which lasts until the wine runs out.

You then set out on a publicity tour of the towns where most books are bought. You give interviews to local newspapers and you appear on local radio and television programmes. This is hard work indeed. You shuttle from one radio station to another to be interviewed by uninterested disc jockeys who have not read your book. As far as they are concerned you are just a filler in between records. I once followed an interview with a woman who wanted to know how to cope with an over-sexed budgie.

It comes as a pleasant surprise when you meet an interviewer who has read the book and tells you he hates it. You can then, at least, have an intelligent conversation.

The technique for these interviews, as explained to me by a veteran of the US publicity circuit, is to give the name of your book at the beginning and then mention it as often as possible throughout the interview.

You will return from a week of this absolutely hating your book. Never mind, you don't have to write another one. Or do you? I find it rather like being a war correspondent. I have to go on just one more mission.

15 KEEPING WITHIN THE LAW

Very early in my career I wrote a story which showed an MP in a bad light because I reported that he had become a director of a German company producing goods in direct competition with factories in his own constituency. My evidence for this was the company's letterhead which named him as a director. He denied the story and threatened to sue for libel. When challenged about the letterhead he said that he had undertaken talks with the company on behalf of his constituents but was not a director and have not given permission for his name to be used in this fashion.

I was convinced that I was right but rather than incur the expense of a trial, the newspaper decided that it was cheaper to pay him the £100 he was demanding. Perhaps I was lucky this happened so early in my professional life and its cost was minimal for I have never forgotten the lessons this taught me.

The first is: check and check again and again. Do not be satisfied with seemingly incontrovertible evidence until it has been cross-checked and proved. The letterheading was not sufficient. I should have confirmed his appointment with the company and then got his reaction.

The second is: journalism is full of pitfalls and traps for the unwary. They are cunningly hidden in the jungle so wrongly named the freedom of the press.

There is libel and contempt of court, there are D Notices and the Official Secrets Act, there is plagiarism and quotes, there is the Press Complaints Commission and the codes of conduct of the National Union of Journalists and the Institute of Journalists, and there are all the 'isms': racism, agism, heightism, handicapism and, most dangerous of all, feminism. There is also a curious new type of trap being imported from the USA which covers most of the 'isms'. It is called 'PC' or 'Politically correct' and must certainly be taken into account when writing for US publications.

LIBEL: THE TRAPS

Of all the dangers, libel is the one that runs through every story a journalist writes and knowledge of the possibility of libel must become second nature to anyone earning their living by writing.

I do not intend to write at length about the intricacies of libel law because it is very well dealt with in other books which should be part of every freelance journalist's library. McNae's *Essential Law for Journalists* (Butterworth) and Tom Crone's *Law and the Media* (Heinemann) are the best examples.

There are, however, certain common sense rules which every freelance should remember. The first, as I have already pointed out, is to be absolutely sure of your facts; but it is not good enough to be sure, you must also be able to prove that what you write is the truth.

You must also take care that you do not draw libellous conclusions from a set of proven facts. A man who calls himself Adolf Hitler, grows a toothbrush moustache and gives the Fascist salute is not necessarily an anti-Semite. It is quite likely that he is but you cannot draw that inference from the facts that you have. You must have further proof of his anti-Semitism before you can print that charge without risk of libel.

You must also take care that you do not libel by innuendo. In 1958 the late Bill Connor, then Cassandra of the *Daily Mirror*, wrote a column about the pianist Liberace in which almost every sentence accused Liberace of being homosexual without mentioning the word homosexual. It was a fearsome attack. Connor wrote: 'This deadly winking, sniggering, snuggling, chromium-plated, scent-impregnated, luminous, quivering, giggling, fruit-flavoured, mincing ice-covered heap of motherhood' . . . 'He is the summit of sex, the pinnacle of masculine, feminine and neuter, anything he, she and it can ever want.'

Liberace sued for libel; he had to or be labelled homosexual in days when the world was far less tolerant of homosexuality. Liberace denied that he was homosexual and the onus was on Connor to prove that he was. He could not do so and in June 1959 Liberace won the then heavy damages of £8,000 and a fulsome apology. The irony of the story was that Liberace was indeed homosexual and had perjured himself before the court. He died in 1987 of AIDS.

It must be remembered in cases like this that if you attempt to prove the truth of an accusation in court and fail it is held to aggravate the libel.

Another example of the dangers of libel concerns the traitor Anthony Blunt. By the 1970s it had become known in those parts of Fleet Street involved with the 'intelligence community' that Sir Anthony, respected art historian and former Surveyor of the Queen's Pictures, was the Fourth Man in the Cambridge spy ring along with Burgess, Maclean and Philby.

A number of journalists and authors itched to break the story but Blunt had done a deal with the Secret Service: in return for telling all he knew he was promised immunity not only from prosecution but also from exposure. This meant that anyone printing the story would be liable to a libel action from Blunt, safe in the knowledge that the Secret Service would not appear for his accuser. All he had to do was deny the charge. Under English law the defendant has to prove that, in legal terms, the words complained of are true. There is no obligation for the plaintiff to demonstrate that they are false. Neither is it any defence under English law – as it is under the US law – to plead that the defamatory statement was published in good faith and in the belief that it was true.

It fell to Andrew Boyle to blow the whistle on Blunt in his book, *Climate of Treason*, in 1979. Even then Boyle tried to avoid a libel writ by hiding Blunt's identity behind the code-name 'Maurice', but it was obvious to Fleet Street and Westminster that 'Maurice' was Blunt.

Private Eye made the connection in print and Blunt started legal moves but Mrs Thatcher pre-empted him by confirming in the House that he had, indeed, confessed to treachery.

Lord Havers, then Attorney General, later explained what had happened. He knew that Blunt was about to issue a writ for libel but 'in no circumstances was I prepared to see him obtain libel damages – perhaps £100,000 – when we knew he was guilty. But how could the author get the evidence . . . ?' Faced with this dilemma, Lord Havers advised the Prime Minister to expose Blunt.

The traitor was stripped of his Knighthood and disgraced and Andrew Boyle's courage was vindicated but it was a near-run thing and as far as libel was concerned he would almost certainly have lost the case if the Prime Minster had not intervened.

I do not suggest that freelances will be faced by a Liberace or a Blunt very often but these cases illustrate the vagaries and dangers of the laws of libel.

Some publications have a cynical approach to libel. They calculate the possible cost of an out-of-court settlement against the readership appeal of the story and if it is considered worthwhile will print it and get the cheque ready.

It is a highly dangerous policy for a freelance to flirt with libel even if you are convinced you are morally and factually right. You do not have the resources of a national newspaper and one bad case could ruin you for life. I need only cite the case of the £1,500,000 damages awarded personally against Count Nikolai Tolstoy for accusing Lord Aldington of war crimes to make my point.

A newspaper will normally assume the libel responsibilities of a staff writer but this does not necessarily apply to a freelance who has sold the paper a story containing a defamation and you could find yourself named in a libel case with all that you own at risk.

So, unless you are very brave, very rich or very stupid, stay away from the libel courts. *Time* magazine once had a rule that a dot had to be put above every word in a story to signify that it had been checked. It is that sort of care that you should apply to your work. Check your facts. Prove your facts. Acquire supporting evidence from people prepared to go to court on your behalf. Keep records of conversations and, if possible, get them signed. Tape what you can. Keep copies in a safe place.

If the story contains sensitive material make sure that it is 'lawyerized' – read for libel by the publication's lawyer. All national newspapers have a staff of lawyers whose task is to read every story for libel. Sometimes they work in conjunction with a wise old journalist, a 'prodnose' who can often sniff out a hidden libel which evades the lawyer.

Many magazines, however, do not have a full-time lawyer reading for libel. It is important therefore that you draw the editor's attention to a story which may, as they say, 'attract legal attention'. The editor can then arrange to have it read.

It does not pay to try to sneak potentially libellous material past the lawyer for fear that your story will be killed. It is much better to go to the lawyer, point out the problem and discuss with him or her a form of words which will enable the story to be printed without fear of 'attracting legal attention'.

Sometimes even this precaution fails and you will be faced with a court action. A major newspaper will fight such an action if it believes your story to be true but a minor publication without much financial backing might well back down when faced with a writ from a rich and ruthless man who could drive it to bankruptcy by extended and financially crippling legal manoeuvres. Rather than fight and go under they will apologize, pay a negotiated settlement and survive.

Given these dangers, the overriding rule is the one that used to hang over the news room of the old *Daily Express*: 'When in doubt leave it out.'

PROTECTING YOUR SOURCES

Contempt of court is another legal-journalistic minefield which is dealt with comprehensively in the appropriate books and should be studied by all journalists. It is complex and there are areas which remain unclear despite the attempt at clarification by the Contempt of Court Act 1981.

Basically the law relating to contempt is concerned with ensuring a fair trial in a particular case and with the administration of justice generally.

You cannot, for example, give details of a defendant's criminal record before he or she is found guilty and sentenced because that could prejudice the trial; neither can you name a blackmail victim even after the trial has ended because the resulting publicity would deter other victims from coming forward.

While it may be assumed that editors and their lawyers are alert to the dangers of contempt there are certain aspects of the law which are of particular importance to the freelance. You may not interview a juror to find out what went on in the jury room. You may not use a tape recorder in court except by special permission of the court. You may not take photographs in court or in the 'precincts' of the court.

There is another aspect of the contempt law of which all freelances should be aware and that is the question of the right, indeed the duty, of journalists to protect their sources. This right, thought to be absolute by journalists, has never been acknowledged in law. However, it was thought by many journalists that it had not only been acknowledged but enshrined in law by Section 10 of the Contempt of Court Act 1981 which says:

> No court may require a person to disclose, nor is any person guilty of contempt of court for refusing to disclose, the source of information contained in a publication for which he is responsible, unless it is established to the satisfaction of the court that disclosure is necessary in the interests of justice or national security, or for the prevention of disorder or crime.

In fact this section leaves the journalist more vulnerable than ever. It is the judges' interpretation of what follows after 'unless' that does the damage.

Take the case of William Goodwin, a trainee journalist working for a specialist magazine called *The Engineer*. An informant told him a story about a deal being planned by two companies. He telephoned both companies to check the story. The companies promptly took out an injunction against him and *The Engineer* on the grounds that the story would damage their businesses.

The injunction was granted and not a word of the story was printed. One of the companies then asked for a court order to make Mr Goodwin reveal the name of his informant.

He refused and was held in contempt of court. He appealed but the Court of Appeal refused to hear his appeal on the grounds that his refusal to name his source or hand over his notes as ordered by the lower court gave him no right to a hearing.

His appeal to the House of Lords met the same fate with Lord Bridge arguing: 'Why should the House of Lords hear an appeal in these circumstances since he has not the slightest intention of complying?' The Law Lords ruled that the threat of severe damage to the business of the company from a possible disloyal employee overrode a journalist's right to protect his sources under the Contempt of Court Act 1981.

So the honourable but unfortunate Mr Goodwin was fined £5,000 and warned that he had narrowly escaped being sent to prison.

Section 10 would, therefore, seem to offer precious little protection to any journalists who feel honour bound to protect their sources. This is a threat that every freelance should bear in mind when dealing with a 'mole'. He or she may be forced to reveal an informant's name and thereby ruin him, or go to prison.

The publication which prints the story has no obligation to a freelance in these circumstances. This does not mean that you should not use a mole's information. Journalism would die without leaks, and many scandals would never be exposed. What it does mean, however, is that you must be very careful how you use your mole in order not to lay yourself open to a charge of Contempt.

D NOTICES

The freelance should also have an understanding of the Official Secrets Act. The much criticized Act of 1911 with its notorious catch-all Section 2 under which any unauthorized disclosure or receipt of official information was unlawful – even the canteen menu – was replaced in 1989 by a new Act described by Douglas Hurd, then Home Secretary, as an attempt to strike the right balance between public protection and individual liberty.

Despite the government's humiliating failure to prevent the publication of *Spycatcher*, the embarrassing memoirs of the former MI5 agent Peter Wright, no change was made in the official attitude towards members and former members of MI5 and MI6. Disclosure of any information relating to their work remains an offence.

In other areas of the Act, however, the journalist faces less danger than before. For a journalist to be successfully prosecuted under the Secrets Act the prosecution will have to prove beyond reasonable doubt that:

- The information or document has been in the possession of a crown servant or government contractor in his official capacity.
- The journalist knows or has reasonable cause to believe that it has.
- It relates to security or intelligence as defined in the Act.
- The journalist knows or has reasonable cause to believe that it does.
- The information has come into the journalist's possession as a result of having been disclosed to someone without authority by a crown servant or government contractor; entrusted to the journalist in confidence by a crown servant or government contractor; or disclosed, not necessarily to him, by a person to whom it had been entrusted.
- The journalist knows or has reasonable cause to believe that the information reached him by one of these three routes.
- His disclosure was made without authority. (He has a defence that he believed he had authority and had no reason to believe otherwise.)
- The journalist's disclosure has caused damage to the work of the security and intelligence services or is likely to cause such damage or that the information falls into a class or description of information likely, if disclosed, to cause such damage.
- The journalist knew or had reasonable cause to believe when he made his disclosure that it would cause damage or was likely to cause damage or that the information fell into a class or description of information likely, if disclosed, to cause damage.

This would seem to be a formidable set of obstacles to a successful prosecution. At the time of writing, it has yet to be tested.

Any journalist unsure about his position with a particular story under the Official Secrets Act can ask through his editor for advice from the secretary of the Defence, Press and Broadcasting Committee, generally known as the D Notice committee.

This committee, consisting of eleven representatives of newspapers, magazines, radio and television, and four civil servants from the Ministry of Defence, the Home Office and the Foreign Office, was formed in 1912 because editors, even then, found the 1911 Act confusing.

Its work centres round the D Notices issued as guidelines to advise editors in general terms about sensitive matters which, if written about, could be harmful to the nation's security. There are at present eight of these notices and the committee meets twice a year to review the operation of the system and, whenever necessary, to amend the D Notices.

The system is purely voluntary and the committee has no statutory powers to enforce its advice so that an editor can decide not to take that advice.

However, if an editor does so and prints a story which is covered by a D Notice he or she will know that the authorities regard it as harmful to national security and that the editor risks prosecution under the Official Secrets Act.

When the secretary of the committee, normally a retired admiral, is asked for advice on a story – this can happen two or three times a week – he assumes the role of independent arbiter. He consults the relevant department of government and reports its reaction to the editor. He can also suggest alterations, often as minor as the deletion of a name, which will make a story safe. It is then up to the editor to decide whether to run the story or not.

The natural reaction of a journalist to handing over what has to be a hot story to the very people who will want to bury it is one of horror. It is, however, one of the conventions of the D Notice system that once the secretary consults a department about a story, it will make no attempt to undermine it or take out an injuction banning its publication; according to Rear-Admiral William Higgins, secretary when the 1989 Act came into force, 'a ringed fence is put round the story for D Notice purposes.'

Inevitably the act of consultation alerts the authorities and enables them to make plans for its publication. They can attempt to lessen its impact and if they judge that the story breaks the Official Secrets Act they can prepare to prosecute the editor in which case the fact that the committee's advice has been rejected will not help the defence.

It is by no means a perfect system because it amounts to self-censorship by the media and government departments do try to use it to classify stories as detrimental to national security when they are only detrimental to the department concerned and their publication is in the public interest.

For the moment, however, it is the only system we have for dealing with these sensitive matters and it is important for the freelance to understand its workings so that the system can be used to get stories printed rather than have them killed out of hand.

WHOSE WORDS?

Another legal pitfall for journalists is the question of copyright. Once again it is a complicated area of law and some lawyers spend the whole of their working lives dealing with it. From a freelance's point of view, however, it is relatively simple: never use a direct quotation from anybody else's work without giving full accreditation; and never use more than 300 words of direct quotes without permission.

The figure of 300 words is arbitrary. All that the Copyright Act of 1956 says is that there should be 'fair dealing' in the use of quotes but if you stick to the 300 word rule you should not get into trouble.

It is rare that you will ever need more than that amount of direct quotes. The way round the limit is to rewrite what you want to lift from the original piece in your own words. You can do this because, curiously, while an author's words are copyright his ideas are not, even though those ideas and their attendant research often entail far more thought and work than writing the story.

Neither is there any copyright in news. A newspaper that has missed a story can lift the facts of the story from another newspaper but it must rewrite the story because while the facts are not copyright the actual form of words in which the story is written may not be copied.

You can see this process at work almost every night in newspaper offices as the news editor waits for the first editions of the rival papers to arrive and then organizes the coverage of the stories that have been missed, while a sub-editor does a quick rewrite job for the immediate edition.

The fact of the matter is that journalists are always feeding off each other. If you go to a cuttings library and look through a file you can see how different writers have taken an original story or interview and reshaped it over a number of years.

You must take care, however; the original story may have contained a terrible howler, a libel even. When it is possible always do your own investigation.

If you have to 'lift' then make sure that you use more than one source. The cynical maxim is: one source is plagiarism, two is research. But be careful. You must remember that this area of the law is constantly evolving and you will need to keep up with its developments.

Never, ever, do what one author did to me. I opened his latest book on terrorism and found paragraph after paragraph copied out of one of my own books. He had not even done me the courtesy of rewriting it. That, I felt, was not only plagiarism but downright laziness.

USING QUOTES

Quotations of a different sort, direct quotes from interviews, can be a source of trouble. Suppose you conduct an interview with someone, brilliant in their own field, but inarticulate — a soccer star, for example. You will want to use direct quotes from him but what if they are so ungrammatical and disjointed that they hardly make sense? Are you going to use them straight, confusing your reader, making the star look stupid, and yourself inept, or are you going to clean up the syntax?

If you do, you may present a somewhat false view of your subject, but does that really matter if the general sense of the interview is conveyed in an article which might otherwise border on gibberish?

My solution in these circumstances is to clean up the essential quotes without altering their character but to rely as much as possible on reported speech without the quotation marks. It also helps if you get your subject's approval of his 'sanitized' quotes.

What you must never do is invent direct quotes even if they convey the sense of the interview. If you are interviewing a business tycoon or a politician it is quite likely that they will make their own tape of the interview and if you write an unfriendly story with direct quotes which they can prove they never said you will look dishonest and stupid and may lay yourself open to a writ for libel. The point is that those little quotation marks are so uncompromising. Once you have put them round some words you are stating: this is precisely what was said. There is no way out of it; that is what quotation marks mean.

If you want to convey the sense of the conversation in your own words in order to clarify or condense what was said or to make a point, which is perfectly legitimate, do not put your words inside the subject's quotation marks.

If, however, your subject uses a word which obviously means something quite different to what was intended it is permissible to substitute the appropriate word as long as it does not change the sense of what was intended. My advice is that you may gently massage quotes but you must never twist them.

RACISM

We now come to the 'isms', those minefields into which most journalists stray, however unwittingly, at some time in their careers. Racism is, I believe, the only one so far that has been made an offence for which a journalist can be sent to prison. Under the Race Relations Act 1976 it is a criminal offence, 'To publish or distribute threatening, abusive, or insulting matter, likely, having regard to all the circumstances, to stir up hatred against any racial group.'

The Act was designed to combat overt racism and outlaw racial discrimination. It is not likely that any genuine journalist would willingly commit such an offence in print but the effect of the Act is to make it illegal for a newspaper to report a speech made by a racist politician or to print a hard-hitting reader's letter about immigration.

Newspapers must also tread warily in identifying a person by race when race is not essential to the story. For example, if John Smith is arrested for murder he should not be described as being black if his colour has no vital bearing to the story. The anomaly here is that it does not matter if you described other defendents as being Yorkshiremen or Scots or Welsh – but you will get into trouble if you refer to 'Paddies'.

When you are forced by the circumstances of the story to put a racial label on people who were born in this country and have all the duties and rights of British citizens but happen to be coloured, how do you describe them?

One of the problems of journalists in avoiding racial blunders lies in the evolving language of ethnic groups. Some years ago immigrants from the West Indies took pride in being called 'Negro'. Then 'Black' became the accepted description. Now, militants describe themselves as 'Afro-Caribbeans'. In the USA many blacks, proud of their origins, insist on being called 'Afro-American'.

One way out of the dilemma is simply to ask the people you are writing about how they would like to be described. Another way is to say 'whose father came from Jamaica' or 'whose family origins are in Lahore' just as you would say 'whose father came from Melbourne' or 'whose family origins are in the Outer Hebrides'.

It is unsatisfactory and the likelihood is that sooner or later you will give offence. I once wrote a strong piece attacking a Palestinian terror group and received a flood of hate mail not from the Arabs but from Jews who felt that I had insulted Israel in a passing reference to the accidental shooting of a hostage when the Israeli army stormed a hijacked plane.

Faced with such sensitivity there is little one can do except never give racial offence intentionally: by all means attack someone because they are odious or criminal or have written a meretricious book, for all sorts of things but never because of their race, colour or creed. And you must always read your copy carefully to ensure that there is no unintentional insult lurking among your words.

It is now considered that 'golliwog' and 'little black sambo', once an innocent part of growing up in Britain, are racially insulting and new words are constantly being added to the racially forbidden list. For example the word 'burly' has been banned at the University of Missouri School of Journalism because it is 'too often associated with large black men, implying ignorance.'

POLITICALLY CORRECT

Similar sensitivities exist among the other 'isms'. The National Union of Students, for example, objects to phrases like 'blind stupidity' and 'deaf to all reason' on the grounds that they are offensive to disabled people. Homosexuals have become notoriously quick to take offence: the description 'gay' is fine in London where the derogatory 'queer' will produce a flood of angry letters. In New York, however, 'queer' is not only accepted but demanded by the militant gays.

In the USA radical students belonging to the PC – politically correct – movement have codified the sensitivities of minority groups and more than 100 universities have accepted a list of words banned because they are said to be 'oppressive'.

At the time of writing, the PC movement has not yet arrived in Britain although there is little doubt that it will soon cross the Atlantic, causing journalists to look even more closely at their copy. This development is not to be scoffed at. PC has become a powerful force in US media and universities and any freelance wanting to sell in the USA will have to be aware of its influence. There is no point in writing an excellent article if it is going to be rejected because it is not 'PC'.

THE GENDER PROBLEM

There is already no doubt about the power of feminism. I was in El Vino's on that famous day in the 1960s when it was stormed by a group of women journalists protesting about the wine bar's rules that women were not allowed in unless accompanied by men and even then could not stand at the bar. The regulars treated it as something of a joke although most of us were secretly pleased that a blow had been struck against the management's iron discipline.

It was not until some of the women went to court and won the legal right to use the bar on the same terms as their male colleagues that many of us realized just how determined the feminists had become. In fact, the women who use El Vino's are now more equal than the men, for under the strict dress rules still maintained by the management, men must wear a jacket and a tie and will not be served if they are wearing jeans. The only stipulation for women is that they must not wear trousers, however smart they may be. I know of one young lady who, unaware of this rule, walked in wearing a trouser suit and was told politely but firmly that, alas, she could not be served. Luckily she had a raincoat with her so she went to the loo, took off her trousers and put on her raincoat and was served with a smile.

There have always been great women reporters and feature writers and those people who think that women war correspondents are a product of television are mistaken. I remember with great pleasure a day in Israel in 1967 at the end of the Six Day War when Clare Hollingworth of the *Daily Telegraph* lectured the victorious Israeli tank generals on how they should have conducted their battle. They listened to her like naughty schoolboys.

However, I also remember the furore when the first woman sub-editor sat down at the subs table of the *Daily Express*. The chief sub seemed to be on the verge of apoplexy. Now women are not only sub-editors but editors and fill many top jobs on national newspapers.

What the effect of the feminist movement means to the male freelance however, is that he must take care with his language not to offend either his feminist readers or his female bosses. He must learn the new 'gender-neutral' language which was once thought to be a daft invention of radical local councils but by 1991 was being adopted throughout the media.

Style-books have been altered to take account of gender neutrality and in the summer of 1991 journalists working for the BBC were issued with a guide telling reporters to avoid the term 'housewife' in favour of 'shoppers' or 'consumers'. 'Girls' is out; it is thought to be condescending and has to be replaced by 'women'. 'Businessman' must also disappear from scripts along with almost every other description ending in 'man'. 'Chairman' may be replaced by either 'Chairperson' or 'Chair'.

A similar new style book has been adopted by the Centre for Journalism Studies at Cardiff in which 'Manpower' becomes 'Workforce'. 'Manning' becomes 'Staffing' and 'Firemen' will be 'Fire-fighters'.

Most of the new language is absolutely acceptable although I still shudder at calling someone a 'Chair'. There are, however, certain words that do not work. For example they had to admit at Cardiff that they could not find a suitable synonym for 'spinster'. The alternatives 'unmarried woman' and 'single woman' were thought equally sexist.

I must confess to my women readers that I have probably been sexist in parts of this book by referring to 'he' instead of 'he/she' and 'him' instead of 'him/her'. I have not meant to offend; the fact of the matter is that there is no common-gender third-person pronoun in the English language and I simply cannot go through a whole book writing 'he or she', or even 'she or he'. It is ugly and calls undue attention to the writer's feminist correctness. 'What a good boy/girl am I.' This problem has recently arisen because until the advent of 'gender-neutral' language 'he' was accepted as meaning both 'he' and 'she'.

There is a way round this problem and that is by using the plural 'they', 'them' and 'their' instead of 'he', 'him' and 'his'. For example: 'If anyone fiddles their expenses they will be sacked – and serve them right'. This is grammatically wrong because it involves turning a singular pronoun into a plural but it is non-sexist and unless someone invents a brand new set of common-gender third-person pronouns I foresee that it will become common usage.

THE CALCUTT CODE

Following a rash of intrusive stories in the tabloids – the actor Gorden Kaye was photographed as he lay in his hospital bed suffering from severe head injuries after an accident – the government set up the Calcutt Committee to inquire into the invasion of privacy by the press. As a result of that inquiry the increasingly ineffective Press Council was scrapped and a new Press Complaints Commission was set up with the threat that if the industry did not put its own house in order the government would impose statutory regulations.

The new Commission, remarkable in that it had some notable poachers turned gamekeepers among its members, adopted a code of conduct drawn up by a working party of eleven editors. Every freelance should have a copy of this code for it contains a number of sections which affect the way we go about our business. You will see that they echo many of the themes I have discussed in this chapter.

- *Privacy.* Intrusions and inquiries into an individual's private life without his or her consent are not generally acceptable and publication can be justified only when in the public interest. This would include: detecting or exposing crime or serious misdemeanour; detecting or exposing seriously anti-social conduct; protecting public health and safety; and preventing the public from being misled by some statement or action of that individual.
- *Misrepresentation.* Journalists should not generally obtain or seek to obtain information or pictures through misrepresentation or subterfuge. Unless in the public interest documents or photographs should be removed only with the express consent of the owner. Subterfuge can be justified only in the public interest and only when material cannot be obtained by other means.
- *Harassment.* Journalists should obtain neither information nor pictures through intimidation or harassment. Unless their inquiries are in the public interest, journalists should not photograph individuals without their consent; should not persist in telephoning individuals after being asked to desist; should not remain on their property after being asked to leave and should not follow them.
- *Intrusion into grief or shock.* In cases involving personal grief or shock, inquiries should be carried out and approaches made with sympathy and discretion.
- *Innocent relatives and friends.* The press should generally avoid identifying relatives or friends of persons convicted of crime unless the reference to them is necessary for the full, fair and accurate reporting of the crime or legal proceedings.
- *Victims of crime.* The press should not identify victims of sexual assault or publish material likely to contribute to such identification, unless, by law, they are free to do so.

- *Discrimination*. The press should avoid prejudicial or pejorative reference to a person's race, colour, religion, sex or sexual orientation unless these are directly relevant to the story.

This may have been a daunting chapter calculated to put off a young freelance, but the pitfalls are there and if you do not know about them you cannot avoid them. In time you will absorb this knowledge as part of your professional skill and when that happens you will find that the danger flags will pop up automatically when you set about acquiring and writing a story.

When you reach that stage there is one last pitfall to avoid: *Complacency. Never think you know it all. Always check and check again.*

16 HOW TO KEEP ACCOUNTS

Throughout this book I have emphasized the need to keep your finances in order. This may be boring to those of my readers who are certain they are going to become rich and famous without bothering much about the pettifogging details of book-keeping. If you really think like that then good luck to you but I doubt if you will survive as a freelance.

Bank managers and income tax officers do not regard you in any special light because you are a freelance. As far as they are concerned you are just like any other small business. In fact, because you have an income which is often irregular and you do not have physical stock in trade like the butcher, the baker and the candlestick maker they regard you with grave suspicion.

You must, therefore, be immaculate in your accounting. You must keep a record of every financial transaction, every story written, every stamp bought, or you will get into trouble with the Inland Revenue and the VAT man, and your bank manager will be reluctant to come to your rescue. You will also actually lose money from stories you have written but not charged for and expenses you have forgotten.

It is only too easy to dash off a story in answer to a late night telephone request and rely on the newspaper to make the payment automatically. But the news editor who ordered the story could easily forget about it in the heat of producing the paper. If you did not make a record of the story you, too, could forget about it, or, at least, forget about the circumstances – the urgency, the length, the importance – which enable you to make a correct assessment of what to charge. You must also do it quickly; the financial magic of a story swiftly fades once a newspaper has become fish and chip wrapping.

LOGGING THE WORK

The key to an orderly financial life as a freelance is, therefore, keeping accurate records, preferably done at the same time as you write the story.

These records start with a daily log of your activities in which you enter details of stories sold and expenses paid. You can do this either in a diary or on a computer disk. If you use a computer it takes only a few moments to enter the financial details at the end of a story. It can then be transferred to the daily log. If you do keep your log on disk, make sure you have a back-up.

An eccentricity of freelancing that will mystify accountants used to the cost of meat, bread and candles will become apparent immediately for it is often the case when you are writing for a newspaper that you will do the story, deliver the copy and see it printed before you know how much you are going to be paid for it.

Some publications insist on paying a standard rate, say £100 for 1,000 words – although many provincial newspapers pay much less. This system is not satisfactory because it takes no account of the worth of the words. A stunning scoop only 200 words long is obviously worth more than a run of the mill feature of 1,000 words.

If you have something special to sell or you are asked to write a 'special', it is best to negotiate a price before you commit yourself to producing the words, otherwise you place yourself in the hands of the editor who marks up the story for payment. The editor's assessment will be made on the length and the importance of the story. This will certainly differ from one newspaper to another; where news desks are in competition for the best stories from their freelances they will pay more than their rivals. Newspapers can also differ from day to day if different people on the same news desk are assigned to making the payments.

Given these circumstances you will usually not know how much you have been paid until you receive your detailed monthly statement of payments from the contributors' accounts department of the newspaper concerned. After a time, you will have a good idea of how much a certain type of story is worth to individual newspapers. You can, in any case, check your account by telephoning the contributors' accounts department and it does no harm whatsoever to be on good terms with the staff of these departments.

If you feel that you have been underpaid or that an item is missing from your account you should contact whoever commissioned you and make your point. It is usually best to make a friendly telephone call and follow it up with a letter giving the details of the payments you are questioning. For this reason alone it is essential to keep an accurate record of the work you have done.

You should also remember that you should be paid a 'kill fee' for work which has been commissioned or bought but not used. 'Kill fees' are not paid for work sent in 'on spec' or if an editor merely asks to 'have a read' of a story which you are offering. There has to be a definite commitment.

Magazines almost always state the price they are prepared to pay when they commission a story; some adopt the system of paying by the day and they mostly require you to submit an invoice for the agreed amount. What is important is that you should get them to agree to pay you on acceptance of copy and not on publication because that means that you could wait up to six months to get paid and if you have been unwise enough to pay your expenses out of your own pocket – always get an advance for expenses – it could mean that your all-important cash flow would dry up. You would get the money in the end but you could have a difficult time while you wait for it to appear.

I am in favour of sending invoices. It may be tedious but it does keep your records straight and if an editor is dragging heels about paying you there is nothing like a formal invoice for twice the amount the story is worth to sharpen a response. What I would really like to see is a system of fines for late payment. I doubt if this will ever receive official approval but I think freelances are fully justified in imposing their own penalties when editors, full of enthusiasm when they get you out of bed in the early hours to cover a story in a howling storm, lose enthusiasm when it comes to paying.

Consultancy fees are especially prone to being forgotten. This happens when a news desk needs to pick your brains but does not need you to write a story. You must make it clear that 'the meter is running' and take a careful record of the time and terms of the 'consult' for they usually take place with a deadline looming and in these circumstances it is quite likely that the reporter to whom you are giving your hard-won information will forget to make the credit. It will then be up to you to remind the news desk and, if necessary, send in an invoice.

There was a time, in those free and easy days when printers in Fleet Street were signing their pay chits 'Donald Duck' and 'Mickey Mouse', when many freelances opted to be paid in cash, and bundles of notes would be handed over to 'an informant' over a glass of beer in a pub. They would only be small bundles but no records were kept of the transaction and the freelance could declare what he liked to the income tax man.

Those days are long gone. The tax man and even more dreaded VAT man have brought Fleet Street to heel. Now it is even becoming rare to be paid by cheque. If you are a regular contributor your monthly account is usually paid directly into your bank. A record is kept of all your payments and dutifully passed on to the Inland Revenue.

THE TAX MAN

Given that you cannot avoid the tax man the next best thing is to use his own rules in a quite legitimate way to cut your tax bills. To do this you need the services of a good accountant, preferably one who specializes in freelance business. I know it costs money to have an accountant but it saves money in the end.

Your accountant cannot, however, cut your tax bill simply by waving a magic pocket calculator. Your help is needed in supplying every scrap of information about your business expenses. Your accountant cannot claim unless your receipts are there to prove that what you say is true. The tax man will accept some estimates of expenditure – taxis, for example – but is much happier with a sheaf of receipts.

Armed with these, your accountant will be able to claim relief under a number of headings. Among them are the accountant's own fees, travel in the course of work, telephone, postage, office equipment, payments to your family for assistance, and the purchase of reference books. Your accountant will thus be able to reduce your tax bill considerably – but only if you are able to supply him with the information needed.

The tax man will then make his assessment and present you with his bill. You pay it in arrears instead of by Pay As You Earn with a company accountant taking the money out of your pay cheque before you get your hands on it. Instead, you have to cough up two large cheques, one in January and one in July. The danger here is obvious: you have been paid by your various clients and the temptation is to put it all into your current account for general use. That way lies disaster because when you have to pay your tax you might find you have already spent it and even if you manage to pay it you will be on short commons for some time.

So it is much more sensible to estimate how much tax you will need to pay on each month's account and put that amount in a building society or post office savings account. In that way you will not spend it 'accidentally' and it will be earning interest – which will of course be taxable – until the time comes to pay the bill.

I know that the temptation to break into the tax account will be too much on occasions when your current account is miserably low but if you can resist you will find that it takes the pain out of paying the tax. It also enables you to pay up promptly. The last thing you want is an irate Inland Revenue inspector mounting a major probe into your finances. He may find nothing untoward but it is time-consuming, worrying and expensive.

THE VAT MAN

It is even more important that you adopt this technique of putting money aside when you become 'vattable' for then you are not dealing with your money which is taxable, you are dealing with the government's money which has been passed to you by your clients for transfer to Her Majesty's Customs and Excise. It is not your money at all, so do not touch it. You can, however, put it in one of the savings accounts where it will earn money for you until the time comes for you to hand it over. The interest you earn on it will be taxable but not Vattable.

The interest is welcome but what is important is that you should not regard the VAT payments as part of your income. As VAT is now 17½ per cent on all the fees and royalties you earn in this country this can reach a tidy sum in three months and if you have spent it you may find yourself in a great deal of embarrassment. The Customs men expect payment on the nail and if you cannot pay up you will leave yourself open to prosecution and heavy sentences. You might chance your luck and argue with the tax man but when the VAT man cometh my advice is to surrender.

You become liable to VAT if:

1 at the end of any month the value of the taxable supplies you have made in the past twelve months has exceeded £35,000,
2 at any time there are reasonable grounds for believing that the value of the taxable supplies you will make in the next thirty days will exceed £35,000.

Once you have registered and been given your VAT number you have to inform all your clients and they will automatically add 17½ per cent to your payments. You will then pass on the VAT money to HM Customs and Excise with the form which will be sent to you every three months. If you wish, you can make arrangements to pay your VAT annually instead of quarterly.

It is a bore to act as the government's tax collector, but the form has been considerably simplified and if you get your accountant to give you a lesson on how to fill it in, it should not take you more than an afternoon. The trick is to keep a running account of your VAT on your computer so that it is a simple matter to make your calculations. Remember that all foreign earnings are exempt and so are payments made under the Public Lending Rights system for any book you may have in public libraries. These payments are calculated on the number of times your book is taken out from a selected group of libraries. You must, of course, remember to register your books for PLR.

There are also legitimate charges that you can make against VAT. You can, for example, deduct all VAT on office equipment and car repairs. You can charge a proportion of the VAT levied on telephone bills and petrol. You can also deduct the VAT on the entertainment of foreign clients. The VAT on your accountant's fees is also deductible. Your accountant should advise you if any of the constant changes in the regulations affect you. If you find the calculations impossible to handle, then hand everything over to your accountant. After all, if you are earning enough to qualify for VAT you should be able to afford one – as long as you keep a proper account of your income and expenses.

WORKING TO A BUDGET

What you have to aim for when you have taken care of your tax and your VAT is a regular income with a reasonable 'float' to cope with emergencies and to finance projects. It is extremely uncomfortable trying to run a freelance business with your nostrils only just above the water. Prudence is the watchword.

Prudence also entails ensuring your future. Staff journalists have office health and pension schemes to look after their old age and any bouts of ill health. Freelances have to make their own arrangements. Too often, when people set out, young and sprightly, on the freelance path they neglect to make provision for old age or ill health until it is too late.

The joy goes out of freelancing if you fall ill and have no insurance to pay the mortgage and buy the groceries, neither is it amusing to contemplate old age with only a State pension between you and penury.

So consult your accountant and take out whatever insurances and pensions you calculate you will need if disaster strikes. You may of course want to go on working until you die, but it is nice to know that you can give up if you want to.

All this means that you have to make a budget. Certain sums must be put aside each month for tax and VAT and pensions and to replenish the float. The rest you can spend on good living like paying the mortgage, school fees, housekeeping, hire purchase on the car and, possibly, a half bottle of sherry.

Remember the words of that great freelance Charles Dickens: 'Annual income twenty pounds, annual expenditure nineteen nineteen six, result happiness. Annual income twenty pounds, annual expenditure twenty pounds nought and six, result misery'.

17 THE TOOLS FOR THE JOB

One of the attractions of being a freelance is that your basic equipment need cost you hardly anything. At a pinch you can run your business with a pen, some paper and a telephone, using the 0800 freephone numbers to dictate your stories to newspaper copy-takers and posting your magazine stories. A second-hand typewriter should be your next acquisition and you should hang on to it even when you have become fully computerized for you never know when the electricity will go down and you will be unable to use all your micro-chip gadgetry.

The more sophisticated your equipment, the more vulnerable you are to disaster. When the great storm swept across southern England in 1987 I was without power for nearly two weeks and my electronic office was useless. I dug out my battered old portable which has seen service all round the world and, although it has a couple of wonky keys, it saw me through the emergency – which provided me with some excellent copy on how people coped with disaster. We may never see another hurricane like that again but there will be other emergencies and it is always prudent to have a fail-safe system.

Some writers prefer to stay with their ancient 'steam' typewriters because these machines have become part of their working routine, they feel their words taking shape through the keys; others have moved on to electric typewriters which give the same feeling of intimacy without the hard work.

Others have taken the next step towards the electronic office and use word processors which enable them to correct and save passages without making the final transition to the personal computer which, for all its efficiency, is a soulless machine, unforgiving when you make a mistake.

THE PERSONAL COMPUTER

No journalist will forget that appalling moment of switching off the computer without pressing the save buttons and seeing a whole day's work lost for ever; or the occasions when the save buttons were pressed but the computer refused to accept the order because the disk was full. It happens to everybody.

The personal computer is, nevertheless, the most important piece of machinery in the modern freelance's office. Most newspapers now have a direct input system for copy and prefer their freelances to use it rather than dictating, posting or faxing copy for the simple reason that it saves money by cutting out a costly step in the production process. Dictation has to be put into the system by copy-takers who have to be paid. Typescript and faxes have to be transcribed by secretaries who also have to be paid. It is also far quicker: a story which can take half an hour to dictate takes just a couple of minutes to be fed automatically into the system over the freelance's telephone line, which is an advantage to the freelance as well as the newspaper.

To work this system, you need a personal computer, a printer, the appropriate software, a telephone and a modulator–demodulator, commonly called a modem, a little box of electronic tricks which plugs into your computer and when you tell it to, gathers up the words you have written on your computer, processes them and sends them down the telephone line into the newspaper's system.

Each system has its peculiarities and you will need to talk to the 'systems editor' at each newspaper to make sure your equipment is compatible and to learn the numbers to call and the procedure to adopt once you have been connected to the system.

In a typical system you will 'log on' by entering your name and password which you must keep secret. If it works properly you will get a message back on your screen saying 'log on complete'. You then enter the code for whichever department your story is destined. The newspaper's computer should then reply something like 'begin file transfer.' You can now send the message over following the instructions of your own computer.

It sounds complicated but once you have got the hang of it, it becomes routine and your copy will wing its way into the system cheaply and quickly. The connection between your personal computer and its big brother has other advantages. Messages can be given and received. You can 'talk' on the machine.

You might also, by arrangement with the systems editor, be allowed to tap into databanks used by the newspaper if the purpose of the story warrants it.

The other great advantage of using a personal computer is that it can also act as a library and retrieval system giving a faster and more efficient service than a filing cabinet. What you have to remember is that a computer is only as good as the person who serves it. It can give you nothing back unless you put the material into it. You must also remember to take a copy of all the material you have stored on disk and keep the copies in a safe place just in case you have a fire or burglary or catastrophic failure of your equipment.

From the point of view of the writer the 'PC' is marvellously flexible. My floor is no longer covered with screwed up pieces of typing paper. If I don't like what I have written I simply delete it, change words or move paragraphs around. Polishing a story does not entail tearing up what you have written, or scribbling in between the lines; you edit on the screen, word by word.

In fact, one of the temptations that must be resisted when using a computer is obsessive correcting, making alterations because they are so easy to do but which do not improve the story and which one would not contemplate if it involved putting a new sheet of paper in the typewriter.

While the computer–modem combination is the most efficient way of getting copy to a newspaper there are still many publications which do not have direct input systems. For these, the fax machine is ideal. It is fast and reasonably cheap and can be set to receive messages while you are out or asleep. There are a number of different types of varying sophistication and price. You will have to decide what suits your needs and your pocket. There are two main disadvantages to the fax:

- The copy that comes off the printer tends to fade and is therefore not suitable for filing.
- You are liable to get junk faxes coming through your machine just as you get junk mail through your letter boxes.

RECORDING AND MONITORING

Tape recorders are essential in the electronic office, one for slipping into your pocket for interviews and making notes and the other attached to your telephone for recording conversations. Your telephone will of course be fitted with one of those answering machines which can be interrogated from another number when you are away from base.

You must have a television set with the Ceefax and Oracle news services to keep you abreast of developing events. It always impresses editors when they telephone about a breaking story and find that you already know about it and have material prepared. Following the success of the CNN 24-hour news service during the Gulf War, many journalists have invested in a satellite dish to pick up the CNN service and Sky's half-hour long news programmes which are broadcast 'every hour on the hour'.

If you are specializing in current affairs, this on the spot television coverage will provide you with background, a whiff of actuality – you can see the events which you might be commenting on – and keep you up to date. For example you might be expert on the effect of a certain course of action but you may not know what the originator of that course of action looks like. The television cameras focused on him many miles away will provide you with the material for an instant and accurate description.

A radio receiver is also an important tool. I find the World Service especially useful for it provides news and background and informed discussion about World events. If your interests lie closer to home, however, you might like to have it purring quietly, tuned to your local station so that you can pick up the news flashes.

YOUR OUTSIDE KIT

The next array of equipment you have to consider is your outside communications kit. For many reporters a mobile telephone is not just a 'yuppie's toy' but a vital piece of equipment putting them instantly in touch with their office. On a stormy night with all the public phoneboxes vandalized it can make the difference between a scoop and a missed edition.

The advances in this form of communication, based on miniaturization and satellites, are quite staggering. In 1991 Singapore Airlines announced plans to equip long-haul airliners with a satellite telephone system allowing passengers to make calls in mid-flight. The next planned advance is for passengers to board planes with a piece of handluggage that will allow them to transmit and receive worldwide by satellite.

The advantages of being able to send copy by satellite were displayed in the Gulf War where reporting teams armed with a portable satellite dish were able to get their copy out much to the chagrin of those relying on telephone lines which were destroyed by the bombing.

In most situations, however, the 'laptop' mini computer serves very well to feed your copy into a newspaper system. The laptops, powered by batteries or by using a power point in your hotel room, have modems which are either built into the machine or plugged into designated sockets.

To use them you attach leads to a telephone receiver, dial the appropriate number and go through the same procedure as you would with your personal computer.

If you are abroad where the telephone plugs are not the same size you have to attach 'acoustic couplers' to the telephone receiver. This takes a little time so to avoid causing chaos on the switchboard it is wise to get one of the small bottles out of the room's mini-bar to hold down the cradle until you have finished your electronic manipulations. The mini-bottle is just the right size for the job. When you have finished you can put it back, or drink to a job well done.

One thing to remember about laptop operations is that you cannot reverse the charges on the call. You will have to pay for the telephone time.

Once again, you will make your choice according to your pocket and your needs. I would not attempt to advise you on what to buy; the technical advances in this field are so rapid that by the time this book appears any advice I give could be out of date.

PHOTO-JOURNALISM

One piece of equipment every electronic office should have is a camera. I always carry an idiot-proof 35 mm camera in my pocket when I go on a story, not in the expectation of getting a photographic scoop but in the sure knowledge that if I did not have the camera with me, a marvellous picture would present itself.

I do not, however, think in terms of pictures for I know that if I do, my reportage will suffer. I cannot do both things at the same time. Other freelances look on picture-taking as a far more important part of their business and equip themselves with a variety of cameras and lenses. Those that specialize in filming the Royal Family and movie stars from a distance to get the unguarded shot have lenses ranging from 300 mm to the monster 800 mm complete with doublers and double-doublers to increase the focal length. The range of equipment is enormous and costly.

A word of warning: if you are going into a war zone remember that a long lens looks remarkably like a gun; one photographer I knew was shot and killed in the Six Day War because he appeared to be aiming a weapon at a group of soldiers.

Getting the picture can become obsessive; it is as if photographers forget all the dangers once they have their cameras pointing at a target even though that target is pointing a real gun at the photographer.

The lengths to which some photographers will go to get '*the*' picture became hilarious at Elizabeth Taylor's eighth wedding in October 1991 when photographers, barred from the ceremony, used hot-air balloons and helicopters to hover over the scene. One intrepid 'snapper' arrived by parachute with a video camera attached to his helmet. He landed only twenty feet from the minister conducting the ceremony.

It was a good try but he was arrested and hustled away without his pictures. Another, flying a paraplane, a parachute with an engine, crash-landed. He walked away unhurt but without a picture. It is estimated that one snatched picture of the ceremony would have been worth $50,000 so possibly their efforts were understandable but it is not likely that paraplanes or hot-air balloons will ever become part of the freelance's everyday equipment.

Young freelances with an interest in photography might do better to try to emulate the members of the small but distinguished band of photo-journalists who are equally competent with the camera and the pen and specialize in photographic essays. Their work, usually from faraway places, commands much space in magazines and fetches excellent fees. These are the men and women who, for example, will take off to Outer Mongolia, spend a couple of months living with the herdsmen and get a dozen pages in *Reader's Digest*. They are highly regarded not only by the news and features magazines but also by commercial organizations who pay fat fees to have their businesses handsomely portrayed by top photo-journalists.

If you do decide to concentrate on photography then your office will take on a different shape because you will need a dark room and an array of camera equipment in addition to your other journalistic equipment.

The great danger in accumulating this arsenal of electronic wizardry is that you may be taken over by it. You can go on buying pieces of photographic equipment and ever more sophisticated additions for your computer until they rule your life.

You must remember that this equipment is only a collection of tools. Its only purpose is to help you function as a freelance journalist. You may well take pleasure in your mastery of the micro-chip but you must not allow the micro-chip to become more important than the word. It is what you write that matters not what you write with.

The essence of the electronic office is that it enables you to gather information, write it, store it and send it out. Any equipment which plays no part in this process is not worth acquiring.

As in every other aspect of journalism your office watchword must be: keep it simple.

ENVOI

You may think, if you have waded this far through my admonitions, that I have been a mite heavy-handed, that there cannot be quite so many dangers lying in wait for the unwary freelance. Don't you believe it. Everything that I have warned you about in this book has happened to me or freelance friends of mine.

The truth is that freelancing is not for faint-hearts or for those expecting an easy ride. If that is what you want then you should get a no-responsibility job on a quiet provincial newspaper and count the days until your pension arrives. There is nothing wrong with that except that you will miss the excitement, the thrills and spills of being a freelance.

If you follow the rules, you can have that excitement and make a decent living out of working for yourself. As I said at the beginning, the ultimate joy of being a freelance is the ability to say 'No'.

Those of you who decide to go freelance have my best wishes. Remember: check every word, make sure your books add up, keep your head down when the shooting starts, write it simply and elegantly and have fun.

Me? It's a fine day. I've switched off the computer and I'm going fishing.

APPENDIX: CODE OF PRACTICE FOR THE PRESS

The following is the Press Complaints Commissions Code of Practice for the Press as revised on July 1993:

The Press Complaints Commission is charged with enforcing the following Code of Practice which was framed by the newspaper and periodical industry and ratified by the Press Complaints Commission in 1993.

All members of the Press have a duty to maintain the highest professional and ethical standards. In doing so, they should have regard to the provisions of this Code of Practice and to safeguarding the public's right to know.

Editors are responsible for the actions of journalists employed by their publications. They should also satisfy themselves as far as possible that material accepted from non-staff members was obtained in accordance with this Code.

While recognising that this involves a substantial element of self-restraint by editors and journalists, it is designed to be acceptable in the context of a system of self-regulation. The Code applies in the spirit as well as in the letter.

It is the responsibility of editors to cooperate as swiftly as possible in PCC enquiries.

Any publication which is criticised by the PCC under one of the following clauses is duty bound to print the adjudication which follows in full and with due prominence.

1 ACCURACY

(i) Newspapers and periodicals should take care not to publish inaccurate, misleading or distorted material.

(ii) Whenever it is recognised that a significant inaccuracy, misleading statement or distorted report has been published, it should be corrected promptly and with due prominence.

(iii) An apology should be published whenever appropriate.

(iv) A newspaper or periodical should always report fairly and accurately the outcome of an action for defamation to which it has been a party.

2 OPPORTUNITY TO REPLY

A fair opportunity for reply to inaccuracies should be given to individuals or organisations when reasonably called for.

3 COMMENT, CONJECTURE AND FACT

Newspapers, while free to be partisan, should distinguish clearly between comment, conjecture and fact.

4 PRIVACY

Intrusions and enquiries into an individual's private life without his or her consent, including the use of long-lens photography to take pictures of people on private property without their consent, are not generally acceptable and publication can only be justified when in the public interest.

Note – Private property is defined as any private residence, together with its garden and outbuildings, but excluding any adjacent fields or parkland. In addition, hotel bedrooms (but not other areas in a hotel) and those parts of a hospital or nursing home where patients are treated or accommodated.

5   LISTENING DEVICES

Unless justified by public interest, journalists should not obtain or publish material obtained by using clandestine listening devices or by intercepting private telephone conversations.

6   HOSPITALS

(i)   Journalists or photographers making enquiries at hospitals or similar institutions should identify themselves to a responsible official and obtain permission before entering non-public areas.

(ii) The restrictions on intruding into privacy are particularly relevant to enquiries about individuals in hospital or similar institutions.

7   MISREPRESENTATION

(i)   Journalists should not generally obtain or seek to obtain information or pictures through misrepresentation or subterfuge.

(ii) Unless in the public interest, documents or photographs should be removed only with the express consent of the owner.

(iii) Subterfuge can be justified only in the public interest and only when material cannot be obtained by any other means.

8   HARASSMENT

(i)   Journalists should neither obtain nor seek to obtain information or pictures through intimidation or harassment.

(ii) Unless their enquiries are in the public interest, journalists should not photograph individuals on private property without their consent; should not persist in telephoning or questioning individuals after having been asked to desist; should not remain on their property after having been asked to leave and should not follow them.

(iii) It is the responsibility of editors to ensure that these requirements are carried out.

9   PAYMENT FOR ARTICLES

(i)   Payments or offers of payment for stories, pictures or information should not be made directly or through agents to witnesses or potential witnesses in current or criminal proceedings or to people engaged in crime or to their associates – which includes family, friends, neighbours and colleagues – except where the material concerned ought to be published in the public interest and the payment is necessary for this to be done.

10   INTRUSIONS INTO GRIEF OR SHOCK

In cases involving personal grief or shock, enquiries should be carried out and approaches made with sympathy and discretion.

11   INNOCENT RELATIVES AND FRIENDS

Unless it is contrary to the public's right to know, the Press should generally avoid identifying relatives or friends of persons convicted or accused of crime.

12   INTERVIEWING OR PHOTOGRAPHING CHILDREN

(i)   Journalists should not normally interview or photograph children under the age of 16 on subjects involving the personal welfare of the child, in the absence of or without the consent of a parent or other adult who is responsible for the children.

(ii)   Children should not be approached or photographed while at school without the permission of the school authorities.

13   CHILDREN IN SEX CASES

(1)   The press should not, even where the law does not prohibit it, identify children under the age of 16 who are involved in cases concerning sexual offences, whether as victims, or as witnesses or defendants.

(2) In any press report of a case involving a sexual offence against a child -

(i) The adult should be identified.

(ii) The terms 'incest' where applicable should not be used.

(iii) The offences should be described as 'serious offences against young children' or similar appropriate wording.

(iv) The child should not be identified.

(v) Care should be taken that nothing in the report implies the relationship between the accused and the child.

14 VICTIMS OF CRIME

The press should not identify victims of sexual assault or publish material likely to contribute to such identification unless, by law, they are free to do so.

15 DISCRIMINATION

(i) The press should avoid prejudicial or pejorative reference to a person's race, colour, religion, sex or sexual orientation or to any physical or mental illness or handicap.

(ii) It should avoid publishing details of a person's race, colour, religion, sex or sexual orientation, unless these are directly relevant to the story.

16 FINANCIAL JOURNALISM

(i) Even where the law does not prohibit it, journalists should not use for their own profit financial information they receive in advance of its general publication, nor should they pass such information to others.

(ii) They should not write about shares or securities in whose performance they know that they or their close families have a significant financial interest, without disclosing the interest to the editor or financial editor.

(iii) They should not buy or sell, either directly or through nominees or agents, shares or securities about which they have written recently or about which they intend to write in the near future.

17 CONFIDENTIAL SOURCES

Journalists have a moral obligation to protect confidential sources of information.

18 THE PUBLIC INTEREST

Clauses 4, 5, 7, 8 and 9 create exceptions which may be covered by invoking the public interest. For the purposes of this code that is most easily defined as:

(i) Detecting or exposing crime or a serious misdemeanour.
(ii) Protecting public health and safety.
(iii) Preventing the public from being misled by some statement or action of an individual or organisation.

In any cases raising issues beyond these three definitions the Press Complaints Commission will require a full explanation by the editor of the publication involved, seeking to demonstrate how the public interest was served.

Comments or suggestions regarding the content of the Code may be sent to the Secretary, Press Standards Board of Finance, Merchants House Buildings, 30 George Square, Glasgow G2 1EG, to be laid before the industry's Code Committee.

INDEX